The Living God

René Voillaume

THE LIVING GOD

Translated by Dinah Livingstone

Darton, Longman & Todd
London

First published in Great Britain in 1980
by Darton, Longman & Todd Ltd
89 Lillie Road, London SW6 1UD

Translation © 1980 Darton, Longman & Todd Ltd

Originally published in French as
L'éternel Vivant by Les Editions du Cerf, Paris
© Les Editions du Cerf, 1977

ISBN 0 232 51431 3

Printed in Great Britain by The Anchor Press Ltd
and bound by Wm. Brendon & Son Ltd,
both of Tiptree, Essex

Contents

Preface

The theme of the following meditations is the personality of Jesus Christ, Son of man and Son of God, in the state of 'divine glory' he is in now, by virtue of his resurrection from the dead, and the nature of the reign of his Spirit in the world in the heart of every disciple.

This double reality of man glorified in Christ and the reign of Christ's Spirit is of course at the heart of the christian faith, which would lose all meaning without it.

The current renewal of the Church stresses the liberating quality of the Gospel for the wider human community, and the social, economic and even political implications of it. Thus, it emphasizes the collective aspect of human problems and their solutions. Given the growing complexity of the economic and social structures in industrialized societies, it was inevitable and right that the content of the gospel message should be interpreted at this level of human relationships.

But at the same time societies and Churches also feel a growing awareness of the need to rediscover the meaning of life, the meaning of mankind's destiny and the personal destiny of the individual. Without denying the importance of social and political relationships which link people together for a common destiny, many people feel the need for an absolute, a thirst for the infinite in their own lives, when they have to face suffering, evil and death.

Who is better able to answer these questions than he

who alone had the courage to claim, which no one dared contradict, that he was able to speak of his own knowledge of God his Father, eternal life and the final destiny of man?

This is why it is more necessary than ever for Jesus' disciples to be aware, in their hearts and minds and in the light of their Master's words, of the real and active Presence in their lives, of the living Christ and the reign of his Spirit. This awareness will make their hope a source of strength for action in the world, a source of peace in times of trial, and of confidence and joy in the expectation of what lies beyond the fearful and lonely passage of death—sharing forever, and this time openly, in the transfigured life of Christ, the 'first born from the dead'.

The following talks were given at Rome during a meeting of the Little Sisters of Jesus. But what is said directly concerns the christian life of every baptized person.

Cepie, 11 March 1977

I

'Who Do You Say That I Am?'

Our life with God is both stable and changing. It is stable because God has revealed himself to us and we can find no other foundation for our lives than this God who has come close to us. But it is also a process of change and continual renewal because we ourselves change, we tend to grow old and become set in our ways, when we should always be reviving our youth. Christ in us is like the seed of constant renewal.

We might sometimes be discouraged by our lives devoted to Christ and his Gospel, because the years go by and we find no renewal or transfiguration of ourselves by Christ. We might wonder what it was all for. It is not easy going.

You asked me about our relationship to the person of Jesus. This is of course the fundamental question if we want to live with him, through him and by him. How can we know him? Perhaps the question is naïve because he is God. But he is also human like us. We would like to know what the apostles John or Peter felt about him, their impressions of the personality of Christ their beloved Master. After they had known him as a close friend, they experienced his absence after his ascension. In what way was Christ then still living and present to them, not only in their memory of his words and face, but with a different kind of living, active presence? How certain were the first hearers of the Gospel, Christ's message, that they were living with him, more closely perhaps than when he was

1

with them before his resurrection? Yes, we would like to have been in their place. But I do not quite know if things would really have been so very different for them than they are for us. Because in fact we are in the same situation as the apostles in relation to Christ and his mystery of life.

Penetrating Christ's mystery and finding him can only be done by faith, which is a gift of God. But we have to seek, to try to understand, because we cannot meet Jesus in the same way as the apostles did: time has passed and Jesus, if he lives in his Church, reveals himself through a multitude of witnesses unknown to the apostles. Christ himself remains silent and only appears to us through the men and women who have lived by him, through Doctors of the Church who have tried to scrutinize his mystery, through mystics who contemplate him in the light of faith. We sometimes feel that these people who thus reveal Christ to us, also partly hide him from us, because their witness is always imperfect. But their witness is our only way to meet him.

Who really understood Christ, even among the apostles closest to him? We can be sure that no one really understood him fully, even at his human level. What about Mary his mother? She of all people certainly knew him better than anyone else because he was her son. But she kept her secret.

Jesus appears to us as a face, a man whose character is portrayed by his actions and words reported in the Gospel. We all have a picture of Christ in us, an image that has slowly formed in our memory by meditating on the Gospel. This is Christ as he lived, as he appeared to his contemporaries and disciples, who told us about him. Then we know, with the apostle Paul, that Christ is present in his Church which is his Body. We wonder how this can be possible. What is the nature of Christ's identity with this human Church? Of course, among the realities that reveal Christ, the Church is also considered by many the one that hides him most, almost to the point of betrayal.

Christ lives in the heart of his disciples, in your heart as

2

a baptized Christian, and in the heart of every man that believes in him. What is the nature of such a presence? Is it real? Or is it just a medley of feelings and wishes which gives us the sense of his presence? Is not this presence purely subjective? This is what some people might think. However, nowadays, we accord more importance than in the past, at least the recent past, to the Word of God as given to us in Scripture. We recognize the importance of this Word which reveals the Son of God and we wonder about the nature of the presence of God in his Word.

Of course we cannot imagine these different modes of God's presence, or even Christ's, the Son of man, as he now lives in glory, as we can imagine the different ways in which a human person can be present. Christ is God. What God is, we do not know. No one has ever seen God.[1] Jesus himself said it: 'No one knows the Son except the Father, and no one knows the Father except the Son and any one to whom the Son chooses to reveal him.'[2] Thus we know that there is a revelation of God in Jesus. We also know that Jesus is alive because he has conquered and overcome death by rising from the dead—this is the centre of our faith—and that he lives in the bosom of the Father, but absent from our world and out of reach of human relationships because his humanity has been transformed by divine glory.

The apostles were full of Jesus' promises, longing to see him again, and they remembered eagerly all that Jesus had said about his return. They awaited his return, and this was bound up with their hope for a city to come, the heavenly city, whose sun would be Jesus,[3] the hand that wipes away every tear[4] and the heart to comfort every pain.

---

[1]'No one has ever seen God; the only Son, who is in the bosom of the Father, he has made him known.' (Jn. 1:18; cf. Jn. 5:37–44 and 6:46)
[2]Matt. 11:27
[3]Rev. 21:23 and 22:5
[4]Rev. 21:3–4

Come not for the righteous but for sinners

When I read the Gospel I realize that the people round Jesus were like people everywhere. They were like people today. Most of them came to Jesus to seek an answer to problems that were troubling them. Doctors of the Law saw him as the Master and teacher and they asked him questions about the Law; they often even tried to trap him. When the child Jesus at twelve years of age escaped from his parents and stayed in the Temple, his Father's House, we are told that he questioned the doctors and that they were astonished at his questions and his answers.[5]

Among the people round Christ, there were some who were awaiting the liberation of Israel and saw him as the Messiah, the Son of David, King of Israel. They saw Jesus, in accordance with their idea of the Messiah, as the one who had come to fulfil their hope. Other Jews discussed various subjects with him. Some, like the Sadducees, did not believe in the resurrection or in the existence of angels. The Pharisees, however, believed in the resurrection and in the existence of angels. They discussed both these questions with Christ. The sick who had witnessed his healing powers went to him to be cured.

But those who came closest to him were those who saw themselves as sinners and came to him with humble confidence to be forgiven their sins, like Mary Magdalene. It was because of these people that Jesus in reply to the Pharisees' protest said that he had come not for the righteous but for sinners, just as a doctor is more interested in the sick than in the healthy. The apostles themselves had their limitations in their capacity to understand Christ because of their preconceived idea of the Messiah which they shared with others of their time. Jesus took a lot of trouble to change his disciples' ideas about the Messiah and I do not think he succeeded entirely while he was still on earth. It was only after his resurrection, and probably

[5]Lk. 2:42–7

4

in the light of Pentecost, that the apostles understood at last the true nature of the Kingdom of God. Yes, Jesus was difficult to understand!

When Jesus questioned Nicodemus, who came to him secretly by night, he said: 'Are you a teacher of Israel, and yet you do not understand this?' And he added: 'If I have told you earthly things and you do not believe, how can you believe if I tell you heavenly things?'[6] But in fact most people did not ask Christ about heavenly things, but about other problems that were worrying them. The apostles went as far as they could, according to their faith. Philip said to Jesus: Show us the Father and that will be enough.' The question was naïve but also perhaps deeper than we realize, because no one can tell how well the apostles had come to know Jesus, the man they were so attached to.

Asking Christ the right questions

The same thing happens nowadays. Who asks Christ the right questions? Looking back on the history of the Church we see that Christ has been interpreted, contested, confiscated by some, discussed, rejected by others, but also adored and prayed to by a great number of people.

The Gospel is a book which will also always be scrutinized and interpreted.[7] Exegetes go on and on trying to decipher the exact sense of the words and the meaning of this or that saying of Christ, forcing themselves, sometimes very hypothetically, to discern words attributable to Christ himself in the commentaries on the first catechesis. As for the theologians, who have sought understanding of the faith for centuries, they frequently disagree and never conclude their discussion of Christ's personality.

Then there are the mystics, who have been touched by some ray of Christ's divine glory and tell us about their

[6] Jn. 3:12
[7] 'Behold this child is set . . . for a sign that is spoken against . . . that the thoughts out of many hearts may be revealed.' Lk. 2:34–5

5

secret experience of meeting the Son of God. Of course we realize that even the most honest scholars and even the holiest mystics have never had, particularly in the way they express their experience, more than a partial vision of God's mystery. Because to the extent that they experienced his mystery it was unutterable and incommunicable.

However, innumerable Christians, priests, monks, nuns and laity have followed Christ over the centuries. How many Congregations and Orders there were, not even counting the waves of devotion and the variety of types of spirituality! Monks and nuns are usually seen as sorts of professional imitators of Christ. However, it is obvious that even the holiest ones were limited in their witness. And there were so many different forms of devotion. We know how great the variety was. Vatican II tried to introduce some sort of unity into worship by centring christian life more firmly on the mystery of Easter and the Gospel. Sometimes things have gone from one extreme to the other. Simplification sometimes also meant impoverishment of the life of the Church over the centuries. Perhaps for a time this is inevitable?

So what is Christ's true face? There is no lack of representations of it in all different styles, and commercializations of it which are an affront. But still, throughout all this, Christ does his work of truth and holiness in people's hearts. And then there are also the works and the lives of the saints.

Living as witnesses to his love

Looking at the world today I realize how necessary Christ is to answer the questions most people ask. But still far too often people ask Christ about problems which are not perhaps those which he came from his Father to answer. We do not know how to question Christ, Christ the master of wisdom, Christ the liberator of the poor, Christ the perfect man. He is all this but who is he really? He did not come to do work or initiate actions, however important, that mankind was capable of planning and undertaking for itself.

When we say the Creed, we confess Christ's godhead, we affirm that he is the Son of God. But who is this Son of God for us? And in what way are our lives and our relations with him truly marked by our faith in the divinity of this man, who is the Son of man risen from the dead? These are the questions we should ask ourselves and Christ, in the light of his Gospel, if we want to be faithful disciples of Brother Charles of Jesus.[8]

You have read Père de Foucauld's writings. They too are imperfect. They are strongly marked by his personality. Time has passed and things are expressed differently nowadays. But we know that there was great love in him and that this great love for the person of Christ was not in vain because its genuineness was proved by his whole life. He died of it. There is no greater love than to give your life for those you love.

As for us, are we going to ask Christ our own questions, or ask him what he wants to tell us, answering questions which we would not even be capable of asking of our own accord? For this we need a quiet and listening heart. 'How can you believe if I tell you heavenly things?'[9] Are most people nowadays in a fit state to listen to someone who speaks to them of heavenly things? Are they capable of treating these things as important? Are they capable of understanding Christ? We cannot be truly one of Jesus' friends, or disciples, unless we ask ourselves certain questions about our relations with him. We cannot build our christian lives on fleeting sentimentality or narrow notions. We must be convinced that there is a certain way of life which will bear witness to him. In order to discover it we

---

[8]These allusions to Père de Foucauld are due to the fact that the talks on which this book is based were addressed to groups belonging to the spiritual family of Brother Charles
[9]Jn. 3:12

7

must look constantly to Jesus, while being fully aware that we will never understand him completely.

Unless you become like children

I conclude these preliminary remarks by reminding you of a living example and a word of Christ's. The example is the Virgin Mary. Perhaps of all human beings she understands most deeply Jesus' nature – not just his character but his deep nature, in so far as the Word of God can reveal itself in a human face and by human gestures and words.

We are very familiar with Christ's words but it is not easy to live by them: 'Unless you turn and become like children, you will never enter the kingdom of heaven.'[10] And we might add, what amounts to the same thing: unless we become like children, we cannot know Christ's face.

So when we are thinking of Christ we should not restrict ourselves to a limited number of questions which happen to concern us, and shut out other questions. Many people do, because they are not ready to look at Jesus with total inner freedom, whereas we should realize that if we want to listen to Christ, it is for him to formulate the questions and tell us what he came to do on earth, what he came to bring us and who he is. Otherwise we will be bogged down in our own ideas about him, full of a prioris and we will be unable to listen to him properly. We are very apt to do this. Which of us in reading in the Gospel has not been tempted to pick out the passages and teachings that suited us, and disregard the others? Who can fully accept Christ's words and sayings as they were formulated by him, without leaving anything out? We have a tendency to make ourselves a Christ in our own image, instead of letting him introduce us into his own marvellous world.

[10]Matt. 18:3

8

He who tries to save his life will lose it

Like most Christians, I am not an exegete and I have not got much time to read. I am not up to date with the latest findings in exegesis. However, I am not trying to tell you anything new. I want to invite you to regain contact with Christ in your christian life, so that you may become aware of your vocation as a baptized Christian or perhaps a monk or nun.

Our vocation does not call us to do anything beyond the scope of what a human being should become in order to be himself. Christian life and religious life always remain fully human. We must live it in accordance with what we have received from God and dedicated to him. We must give our lives. Jesus said: 'Apart from me you can do nothing.'[11] We must understand what he is saying because at first sight it looks exaggerated. Of course there are plenty of things we can do without Christ. Some people would even claim that they could do everything without Christ. However, we must take these words of Christ's very seriously. We are always up against the spiritual poverty and impotence of our lives. Do you think there is a single one among us who does not really know how shabby his life is? And those among us who have advanced in age and experience of God would be the first to admit it. Moreover, we cannot approach Christ except in this state of humility, with no illusions about ourselves or our lives.[12] We are constantly proving the truth of Christ's saying: 'For whoever would save his life will lose it, and whoever loses his life for my sake will find it.'[13]

All our meditation on the person of Jesus should be in this spirit of humility. We should broaden our heart and spirit, as an unprejudiced child is able to do. We must be prepared to accept everything, believe everything Jesus says, especially what he says about heavenly things. Our

[11]Jn. 15:5
[12]See the parable of the Pharisee and the publican, Lk. 18:9–14
[13]Matt. 16:25

9

minds must be humble. Faith is the mind's obedience. This is something we find very difficult nowadays. We have faith but we would prefer it not to commit our minds to super-terrestrial realities. This is one of the chief obstacles to faith today. We find it difficult to admit that it demands adhesion to an intelligible content. We think of it more as a general attitude towards life, a feeling, a life style, as the Gospel proposes, directed towards a certain hope whose content we leave rather vague. Of course faith is active, faith which makes us surrender to Christ, faith in a person. We cannot value reflections on the person of Jesus except in the light of faith. We can only know to the extent that we surrender to this truth and let it change our lives. We must 'do' the truth, truth sets us free,[14] and 'sanctifies' us.[15].

[14]'If you continue in my word you are truly my disciples, and you will know the truth and the truth will make you free.' Jn. 8:31–2
[15]'Sanctify them in the truth; thy word is truth.' Jn. 17:17

II

'You Are the Messiah, the Son of God'

How can we speak about Jesus, as he is alive today? This matters to all of us. Père Foucauld's writings show us how much Jesus was the centre of his life, the source of his love, the ultimate goal of his whole existence. This ought to be just as true, in secret, for every Christian who wants to live by Christ. But how can we describe these things from the outside? There is a great difference between the person of Jesus as we find him when we read the Gospel, and him who lives in the heart of each of his disciples, all those who have confessed with profound conviction: 'Truly this man is the Son of God.'[1] That is why Christ remains, and will remain until the end of the world, a subject of debate.

'So who is this man?'

Sometimes I wonder if we realize the importance and seriousness of our faith. We believe that Jesus is God. I do not know how each one of us came to believe this. Of course there are those who have worshipped Jesus from childhood, never had any doubts, so that their christian vocation or their decision to offer their life on earth to him by taking religious vows seems like the normal outcome of the faith they have lived by for so long. For others perhaps

[1]Mk. 15:39

11

there was a conversion, more or less radical. Faith is always a personal happening in the soul, because there are others who have heard of Jesus, or glanced at the Gospel, without this man from past history making any difference to their lives, except perhaps by some of his words. Some may remember that Jesus said we should love one another; others that money is our greatest enemy. Yes, I really wonder if we realize just what our faith means. We must be aware of what an extraordinary thing it is in relation to human life. Faith comes to us from ordinary human life, and we must realize how greatly it ought to transform it. If we embark on a christian or religious life without realizing that we have attached ourselves to a God-Man who should transform our whole existence, then we have not really understood what Jesus has called us to.

Yes, Jesus is a man. That seems quite natural to us, it goes without saying, especially nowadays. Jesus as man has perhaps never been so well known and analysed. Modern exegesis shows us Christ, his personality and environment, with much greater precision and perhaps objectivity than in the past. But this should not allow us to forget that at one time at the beginning of Christianity, it was Christ's humanity that was questioned, because Jesus was seen as God and this led people to say that he was only the semblance of a man. This might seem odd to us today. Because our problem is precisely to confess that Jesus is God. We are so used to saying it, but we should realize fully what a jolt this confession gives to human reason. It jolts reason in two apparently opposite ways. For some who do not believe in God, the statement seems meaningless. In a materialistic and atheist world how is it possible even to ask such a question about an historical man? And if, on the other hand, we take the believing world, such as was the Jewish world with its extremely high and transcendental notion of God, it is impossible to believe how a man could say he was God. Such a statement sounds like a contradiction. The Muslim world in our time still has these same reactions as the Jews about Christ.

But we believe that this man Jesus is our God and that in him death is conquered. We believe that Jesus is a man who suffered death, but whose humanity was then transfigured, illuminated, made eternal, so that he lives on in a way impossible for us to imagine, but which is the foundation not only of our faith, our hope, but also of the Church, the Kingdom of God and the eternal city of the world to come.

We should take stock of the dimensions of our faith, not perhaps because we doubt—although of course that can happen—but because we have grown used to a faith whose seriousness does not always measure up to its object. Faith in us is subject to our own limitations. How can our minds, through faith in Jesus, encompass the very mystery of God? Yes, it is difficult to know Jesus. It is even more difficult to speak about him. The Gospel shows us how many different reactions people had to the man it so soberly describes: the questions put to him by the Pharisees and Sadducees, often merely to trap him; the behaviour of sinners towards him: his attraction for certain religious types. In the whole country there was an aspiration towards a certain notion of a Messiah, which people tended to recognize in Jesus.

As for us, calling Jesus the Son of God may seem obvious in so far as we have acquired a certain idea of the Trinity and the relations between the Father, Son and Holy Ghost. This seems like an acquisition of our faith. So when we say that the Word became flesh, we think of this second person of the Trinity, who became incarnate in Mary's womb and was born as Jesus. But perhaps we forget that this mystery of the Trinity is beyond our comprehension, and that before it was revealed, Jesus Christ came on earth, and that it is only through him that we know of it. This is one of the realities we are in the process of rediscovering: the manifestation of the three persons in the story of Jesus. The Church's meditation, scholarly inquiry into this revelation of the Father by the Son who sends his Spirit, gave rise to a whole theological framework on the nature of a single

13

God in three persons. And we are asked how we can know such things about an invisible God. Theological reflection on the mystery of the Trinity starting from the revelation of the Father in Jesus is an admirable work of the human mind acting with faith. It presupposes the development of the metaphysical dimension of the mind which thus becomes capable, through philosophical insight, of penetrating knowledge of the divine and invisible realities revealed to us by faith. But you know what current difficulties the mind is encountering in its metaphysical capacity. So we come back to the human person of Jesus and ask him again: 'Who are you?'

Jesus, true God, a stumbling block for Israel

To return to this profession of faith in Jesus as the Son of God, it is useful for us to go over the steps the apostles and those Jews that believed in him had to take. The idea of Son of God and Jesus' words which could be interpreted as a statement of his identity as Son, when he said that the Father was in him and he was in the Father, and many others of his sayings on the nature of his relation to the Father, were not very clear to his contemporaries. It is difficult for us to imagine what the name Son of God meant for the Jews of Christ's time.

If we remember this, it helps us to understand the steps the mind had to take to reach the faith that has been given to us. Furthermore, Jesus himself was very reticent on the subject. He did not openly proclaim that he was God. He knew only too well that such a statement would shock the religious mentality of the people and could not be understood. He sometimes suggested it. He did give himself away when he was asked straight out. The same was true of his role as Messiah. When the angel announced Jesus' birth to Mary, he expressed himself in terms which could leave no doubt in the mind of a religious Jew: the angel was talking about the Messiah. And the angel added: 'He shall be called the Son of the Most High.' What could this title mean? When later the Jews accused Jesus of claiming to be God, we know his answer; he evaded the question and neither denied nor affirmed clearly who he was: 'Is it not written in your Law, "I said you are gods"? If he called them gods to whom the word of God came (and scripture cannot be broken), do you say of him whom the Father consecrated and sent into the world, "You are blaspheming" because I said "I am the Son of God?" ' [2] Slowly and gradually the truth dawned on the apostles. Son of God was of course a traditional title of the Messiah. But did that mean he was God? 'What do you think of the Christ?' Jesus asked them one day; 'whose son is he?' They answered: 'David's.' Then Jesus quoted David's messianic psalm to them: 'The Lord said to my Lord . . .' and he added: 'If David thus calls him Lord how is he his son?' That was all. The Gospel simply adds: 'And no one was able to answer him a word, nor from that day did any one dare to ask him any more questions'.[3]

Jesus suggests and reveals his divine origin more by his behaviour, especially towards his Father, the God of Israel, than by declarations of his identity. However, there are moments when we get the impression that among the people, those who have pondered most on Christ's attitudes have attained a real need to know. Then they ask him straight out: 'How long will you keep us in suspense? If you are the Christ, tell us plainly.'[4] In fact Jesus only speaks openly when he is about to die. And even then he merely replies, 'You have said so' to the high priest who adjured him to say whether he was the Messiah.[5] However, he added: 'But I tell you, hereafter you will see the Son of man seated at the right hand of Power, and coming on the clouds of heaven.'

Jesus knew perfectly well that confessing his divinity

[2]Jn. 10:34–6
[3]Matt. 22:41–6
[4]Jn. 10:24
[5]Matt. 26:63

15

would be quite meaningless to a Jew who believed in a God who was the creator, sovereign, infinitely great, of whom it was forbidden to make any image at all and who only spoke to the people through the prophets. The figure of Moses was certainly the greatest in Israel. He was considered by the people as God's close friend who could speak to God face to face. But when he had thus met his God his face shone so brightly that he had to wear a veil in front of the people. How then could they believe that this transcendent God could become identified with a man, be a man?

A political trial?

When we say that Jesus is our God, we proclaim a truth whose import we seldom realize. Either we minimize the idea of God, or, if we believe in his transcendence, we are stating something of immense importance to mankind. How can a man be God? Of course a belief in the absolute character of humanity, and its total independence corresponds to the mentality of our time. Man is God! If Christ was merely a manifestation of this sovereign royalty of man over the universe, then why not?

But we cannot confess Jesus as the Son of God in the full truth of the mystery without at the same time affirming our total faith in the God of Abraham, the God of Moses, the God of Elijah. When we think of the signs given by the prophets, like Moses, like Elijah who raised the dead, and of the place they held in the history of Israel, Jesus' attitude becomes disconcerting. That is why people expect Jesus to do and give something different from what he does. If he is really a great prophet, if he is the Messiah, he should behave differently and reveal himself more clearly. This is what his family tell him: 'No man works in secret if he seeks to be known openly . . . show yourself to the world.'[6]

[6] Jn. 7:4

16

Some people even thought he was not quite sane.[7] Yes, his behaviour was strange because while he revealed himself through signs, he demanded silence on the subject, unlike the prophets who proclaimed themselves to all Israel. The prophets worked signs. Elijah raised the dead. Jesus raising the dead was not therefore abnormal for a great prophet. But he did not behave like a proper prophet. A prophet was someone who proclaimed the Law in the name of God, reminded the people of the obligations of the Covenant which Israel should respect.

John the Baptist was also a great prophet and an exceptional character, in that he was a link between the Old Testament and the New. He was Jesus' forerunner who prepared the way for him. But John the Baptist worked no miracles or signs. His only sign was that everything he said about Jesus was verified by the facts. John gave no signs, but we have to recognize that what he said about Jesus was true. John was just Jesus' forerunner, which was why he effaced himself and worked no signs. But he was a prophet in the strongest sense of the word and remained so till the end: he died for proclaiming the requirements of the Law and for having dared to reproach Herod for taking his brother's wife. For this he was put in prison and beheaded. But what was surprising was Jesus' silence when he heard of this arrest, as if he did not want to be involved with him. He even left Galilee. John must have suffered greatly in prison from Jesus' silence. This is understandable: yes or no? Was Jesus the one he had proclaimed? He ruminated and was tortured by doubts.[8]

Jesus therefore was not a prophet in the great line of the other prophets. Jesus was not put to death for denouncing the injustices of his time, but because he was faithful to the last to his personal identity as Messiah, the Son of God. There is always room for historical discussion on the exact

[7]'And when his friends heard it, they went out to seize him, for they said, "He is beside himself." ' Mk. 3:21
[8]Matt. 11:2–3

17

reasons for his condemnation. Was it for a political reason? Was it because the authorities feared a revolt? Was Pilate to blame because he was afraid that Christ's influence was dangerous to Roman authority? Or was it simply his weariness or opportunism which gave way to the charge brought by the Sanhedrin condemning Jesus in the name of the Law of Moses, because he had blasphemed by calling himself God and was guilty of a capital offence?[9] We do not really know, and probably these different motives were mixed in his trial.

These days we are inclined to stress the political aspect of Christ's trial: he was put to death because he challenged the authorities and by his teaching he attacked established institutions. But it is not as simple as that. Jesus indeed died because of the apparent contradiction between his claim to be the Son of God and the Messiah, as much for the Jewish people as for the political empire of Rome.

In the religious world of Israel, Jesus was a large question mark. To those with a monolithic faith in the transcendence of the thrice holy God of Abraham and Moses, Jesus was a blasphemer. How was it possible to believe that a man is God? In the political sphere he was a Messiah who disappointed the hopes of those who believed in him. This was why it was difficult for the people of his time fully to believe in Jesus. How many did believe? He was indeed followed by crowds, he touched many hearts, but his behaviour was incomprehensible to nearly all of them.

That is why there were so few records of Jesus in the secular history of his time. This in itself is remarkable. His name was barely mentioned, once or twice I think, in the annals of the time. Jesus was not a spectacular man. He did not have a great influence on events, at any rate his influence was much less than that of certain political lead-

[9]'This was why the Jews sought all the more to kill him, because he not only broke the sabbath but also called God his Father, making himself equal with God.' Jn. 5:18

'We stone you for no good work but for blasphemy; because you, being a man, make yourself God.' Jn. 10:33

ers whose names have gone down in history, who took part in the revolt of Israel against the Romans. Some were before Christ and some were after him. In secular history we can more or less say that we find no trace of Jesus.

Is not something similar true of today? The modern world finds it hard to believe in a creator God: this is not our difficulty when it comes to faith in Jesus. He is not rejected because he said he was the Son of God. Whence the tendency to make of the faith a sort of belief in the coming of a new order, a human revolution, proclaimed more or less by Jesus, and whose dimensions can only be earthly, historical and thus political. Because what can we know or believe about things beyond history? Our contemporaries are not interested in questions about this beyond, because they find them pointless or meaningless.

'A spirit has neither flesh nor blood ...'

We have spoken of John and Paul as two great witnesses to Jesus. There are also the other apostles and the evangelists Mark, Matthew and Luke. The historical event is really the faith of the apostles. This is where everything begins. The episode at Caesarea, Simon Peter's profession of faith, was preceded and prepared for by other events. Certain signs worked by Jesus filled the apostles with a sort of holy fear of their Master, like for example the miraculous draft of fishes. Peter's reaction was one of terror. He felt a divine power and that he himself was a miserable sinner. The most intimate disciples had not yet understood. Jesus said to Simon: 'Do not be afraid, I will make you a fisher of men.' This statement of Christ's was very important.

We do not pay enough attention to some of Christ's words. I would like to recall two of his statements. Peter, in reply to Jesus' question: 'Who do men say that the Son of man is? . . . But who do you say that I am?' says, 'You

19

are the Christ, the Son of the living God.'[10] On this occasion the phrase Son of God, which could have just meant the Messiah, the Son of David, meant something quite other for Peter: the truly divine relationship between Jesus and his Father. Jesus stresses the point: 'Blessed are you, Simon Bar-Jona! For flesh and blood has not revealed this to you, but my Father who is in heaven.' Jesus is talking about a personal revelation, not about his Messiahship but his divine Sonship. 'Flesh and blood has not revealed this to you', that is to say not human reason or even human experience. It is a revelation from the Father which Jesus stresses saying, 'but my Father who is in heaven.'

Jesus speaks further of this revelation. This time it is reported by the beloved disciple: 'No one knows the Father except the Son.' And on another occasion Jesus says he speaks about what he knows. He does what he sees the Father do.[11] He alludes to a world from which he has come. He speaks of heavenly things with special knowledge. He says to Nicodemus[12] and on several other occasions, 'Truly no one knows the Father except the Son.' Everything that the prophets had said up till then about God stopped short of the inmost mystery of his Fatherhood, which human beings did not know about and could not know about of their own knowledge. It is a secret mystery. But Jesus adds, 'and anyone to whom the Son chooses to reveal him.'[13]

This means that faith includes a true inner revelation. However anyone comes to the faith, he does not believe by the power of reason alone. And if anyone says to me that the greatest proof of our faith is Christ's resurrection, I reply, no, the resurrection is not the proof of our faith, it is its content. How indeed can we prove that Jesus rose from the dead? We cannot. Paul claims that witnesses saw him risen from the dead and he lists these witnesses. But

[10]Matt. 16:13–20
[11]Jn. 8:38; 14:31
[12]Jn. 3:11–13
[13]Matt. 11:27

20

they are dead now. And anyway how did they experience the risen Christ?

Perhaps you have been shocked like other Christians by the statement of certain exegetes or theologians that Christ's resurrection is not an historical event. Of course this depends on the way in which this statement is understood. You say that it is an historical event, because you believe that Jesus really rose from the dead and that this is therefore a true fact. But what do we mean by saying that Jesus rose from the dead? History can only be an account of earthly things and facts that can be established by experience of them or by the witness of others. In this sense, the only historical fact is that the apostles went to the tomb and that the tomb was empty. And they discussed what this empty tomb could mean. You know the explanation given at the time by the Romans: the disciples had stolen the body of Christ and hidden it.[14] How is it possible to prove this wrong? History can only say that people claimed to have seen Christ alive after his death.

But the experience of the risen Christ is a fact which is no longer of an earthly nature. It cannot be proved on earth. It is a personal or joint experience of some people, and this experience is of supernatural origin. The Risen Christ is in another world. When Jesus appears to the apostles it is to give them a sign, to arouse their faith: 'It is I myself;' says Jesus, 'handle me, and see; for a spirit has not flesh and bones as you see that I have.'[15] It is indeed the same person, the same Jesus, but he is also different. He is no longer an earthly being, although he remains a member of the human race. When Paul says: 'If in this life we who are in Christ have only hope, we are of all men most to be pitied',[16] he is saying that Christ has no meaning for us if he has not risen from the dead, that is to say if he has not founded for human beings, by his deified

[14]Matt. 28:12–15
[15]Lk. 24:39
[16]1 Cor. 15:19

humanity, a world of eternal life which is quite other from this world. At the moment there is a frequent tendency to interpret Christ independently of this eternal dimension, to say that by his teaching and example he established a relationship of love and justice between human beings, a relationship demonstrated by respect for the poor. We can get all this from the Gospel, leaving aside the resurrection, and leaving aside the meaning of Jesus' claim that he was the Son of God, identical with him 'through whom all things were made'.

However, this makes a great difference to the nature of the mission entrusted by Christ to his disciples. What does preaching the Gospel mean? What is the content of the Good News? Jesus said: 'Blessed are you, Simon!' Have we fully realized this blessedness of faith? For it is indeed the first of the beatitudes. Jesus said: 'Blessed are the poor, for theirs is the Kingdom of Heaven', because God's poor are ready to accept the faith. Jesus called Simon blessed because he had received this gift from the Father, because he had had the mystery of the Son revealed to him. Nowadays we would say that the Holy Spirit had enlightened Simon. But the Holy Spirit is also God and we believe in one God. God is also the Father. Jesus speaks explicitly of a gift from the Father. It is the Father who reveals Jesus as God to men. And the Father who reveals the Son to us. That is why Paul says no one can call God 'Abba, Father' except in the Spirit of Christ, the Holy Spirit.[17] Thus the Father reveals the Son to us in our faith, while at the same time the Son reveals the Father.

A presence which divides history into two parts

What happened, what began in history with the death and resurrection of Jesus, which was believed in only by a small group of disciples? What began was really something out-

[17]Rom. 8:14–16

side the scope of history and thus cannot be recorded by it. It was the tiny, almost invisible seed, unseen by history, which Christ sowed in human hearts, and which was the seed of the Kingdom of God. This seed was the smallest of all seeds. The consequences of its sowing are immeasurable. When we say that Christ's coming divides the history of the world and mankind into two parts, this is a reality which only believers can perceive. Of course, we have adopted the custom of counting the years from zero at the presumed date of Christ's birth. This reflects the attitude of christian faith at a certain period. Because what Jesus left behind, even after his resurrection, was in fact an extremely frail reality: a handful of Jews had faith in the man Jesus: they were believers.

Their faith was weak. It was strengthened on the day of Pentecost, but still when Matthew describes Jesus' last meeting with his disciples, at his ascension, he says that some still had doubts.[18] So there was a contradiction in this final meeting: on the one hand there was a small group of followers some of whom were shaken by doubts, and on the other Jesus proclaimed: 'All power has been given to me in heaven and on earth.' All power has been given to me in heaven and on earth! How can he prove this? He had not resisted death. Some of them still remembered what they had heard.

The apostles found it difficult to believe in the resurrection, because this transcendent reality was not of this world. They could not prove it. They had to *believe* that Jesus had risen from the dead because he had risen for and in another life. Otherwise he would be always with them, as he had been before his death. But it was not like that and when he was with them it was not at all the same as it had been before his death. And Jesus continued: 'I am with you always to the close of the age.'[19]

[18]Matt. 28:17
[19]Matt. 28:20

23

How can he be with us? This is the difference, this is what divides history into two parts, the reign of Christ, whose nature is unique because he who reigns is God-man, the man Jesus glorified as God's Son in a state that did not exist before his resurrection. Yes, it was the faith of the apostles which was the new beginning, humble indeed but gradually spreading. For what was the Church then? Just twelve poor apostles and a few disciples—that was all that history could show.

The Kingdom beginning

Sometimes we look back nostalgically on the faith of the first christian community. I think we are prone to illusions about it, as if they too did not have their weaknesses, limitations and deficiencies, just like us. The difference was that this community was the very first band of Christians, alone and isolated, and that its members had known Christ when he was on earth. But we have only to read the Acts of the Apostles to realize that everything did not always go smoothly. The disciples had decided to help one another, but in the help given to widows some were left out. Helpers had to be appointed, the first deacons, to share out the resources and be in charge of community administration, because the apostles could not do everything. And you have not forgotten the story of the Ananias and Sapphira who cheated about the price they got for selling their property.[20]

In this first community, there was also the illusion, which was a kind of weakness, that they expected Christ to return very soon. The memory of the Lord was kept alive among them because many of them had seen and heard him while he was on earth. Jesus had spoken of his return in rather vague terms. He had refused to answer questions about the date of the ruin of the Temple and the end of the Kingdom

[20]Acts 5:1–11

24

of Israel. His preaching about his return was mysterious, and the early Christians found it difficult to become clear about the true nature of the messianic Kingdom so long awaited. When was Jesus going to restore it? Some thought it would be when Christ returned and that this would happen soon.

We cannot help wondering what Christ felt about Israel. They were his people! He was their promised Messiah. Why had his people not recognized him? This rejection also had political consequences. In' fact, what might have happened if Israel had accepted Jesus as the Messiah? Jesus wept over Jerusalem, his city, but he did nothing to avert the disaster coming to it. He wept because Jerusalem was going to be sacked, his people defeated and crushed. Jesus had nothing to do with the organized movements for liberation from Roman domination. He wept.[21] His Kingdom was not of this world.[22]

All this was very difficult to understand for the Jews who had believed in Jesus, and followed him as the Messiah. Something ought to happen, some great event. It was at the very end, when Jesus was about to leave them, that the apostles again asked him: 'Lord, will you at this time restore the kingdom to Israel?'[23] This was a straight question, of supreme importance to the gathering of people who were suffering under Roman rule. Jesus gave no answer! He foretold the ruin of the Temple and the Holy City. The apostles' faith had a long way to go till they understood that the Kingdom Jesus was talking about was not of this world, understood what he did mean about this new Kingdom beginning slowly to grow, the Kingdom of God, the Kingdom of Christ, the Body of Christ. St Paul had very clear ideas about the mystery of the Body of Christ, and he had to fight against the tendencies of the early com-

[21]'And when he drew near and saw the city, he wept over it.' Lk. 19:41
[22]'My kingship is not of this world; if my kingship were of this world, my servants would fight, that I might not be handed over to the Jews, but my kingship is not from this world.' Jn. 18:36
[23]Acts 1:6

munities to expect Christ's swift return. There are even passages where Paul seems to expect this too. That is why everything is transitory, this world will pass away: let him who has behave as if he had not, let him who is married behave as if he were not, let him who has business behave as if he had not, for the form of this world is passing away. Christ is coming![24] Jesus had insisted on his sudden and unexpected return. He would come like a thief when no one expected him.

Yes, our faith is the faith of the apostles, and cannot be anything else, because I cannot see how we can reach Christ, the Son of God, except through the faith of the apostles. What the apostles knew about Jesus comes out most clearly in the gospel of John, who more than anyone else grasped the mystery of Christ. He passionately loved his master, and his confession of Christ's godhead was an insight he passed on to us. John's gospel is certainly the fullest expression of the faith the apostles had in Jesus, a faith later enlightened by the gifts from the Holy Spirit on the day of Pentecost. If we had lived in Jesus' time, it is quite possible that some of us, perhaps nearly all of us, would have listened to him for a time and then abandoned him just like the crowd that followed him at first. Because most of Jesus' followers had a certain messianic ambition and left him in disappointment.

Finally, it is important to remember that our faith is a gift from the Father. However we came to the faith, however weak or deep it may be, it is and remains a gift from the Father. 'No one knows the Son but the Father.' And our faith in Jesus leads us to faith in the Father. Our faith in God would be very limited and weak if it were not lit by the revelation of him that Jesus made. And vice versa, we cannot believe in Jesus without being enlightened and led by the Father. 'No one can come to me unless the Father

[24]'I mean, brethren, the appointed time has grown very short—from now on, let those who have wives live as though they had none, . . . those who deal with things of the world as though they had no dealings with it. For the form of this world is passing away.' I Cor. 7:29–31

who sent me draws him.'[25] There is no direct route to the faith, we cannot get there by reason. Our faith is both fragile and precious. It is often very obscure.

What image can we have of Christ's face and character? Our image is often over-simplified and we must be careful because people go a lot by it. I am not speaking of statues and commercialized images. I mean our way of praying, the form our devotions take, our attitudes which are some-times based on an image which is not truly the Son of God's. We must constantly renew our faith in the light of the apostles'. This is why the gospels and St Paul's epistles are so important. Even if you read them over and over again, these texts are inexhaustible, if you try continually to enter the heart and mind of their writers who bore witness to what they believed. And we in our turn are also witnesses to this faith and these beliefs.

[25]Jn. 6:44

III

The Eternal Living God

Up till now we have tried to follow and understand as well as we can the development of the apostles' faith, their discovery of Christ's character, beyond the bare external impression that any of his contemporaries could have had of him. The apostles' knowledge of Jesus developed to the point where they knew his inner self as Son of God.

This discovery, precisely because of its immensity, was not completely fathomed by the apostles. I do not think this is possible for any human heart or mind. The apostles had lived with their Lord for three years, they had seen his miracles, loved him deeply, and venerated him as their Master. They had no other. They had never met anyone who spoke to them like Jesus and they were convinced that he was the Messiah foretold by the prophets and awaited by Israel.

Jesus led them to the point where they confessed (in the person of Peter), his divine Sonship. But were they fully aware of the implications of such knowledge? We doubt it, because at the time of the Passion, their attitude showed that they had not yet truly understood the meaning of what was happening.

'It is good for you that I am going away'

At the beginning of the Acts of the Apostles the author returns—not unintentionally—to the temporal messianic perspective which continued to dominate the apostles. Jesus had undergone the Passion, the utter defeat of the messianic kingship, its ultimate failure through the death of him who was to have liberated Israel. They had seen Jesus risen from the dead and at first they had doubted. Then their hearts had spoken and they had believed. And yet on the mountain in Galilee at the very moment when Jesus was about to leave them, the apostles again asked him: 'Lord, will you at this time restore the kingdom to Israel?'[1] The events that had happened had reminded them of all the Old Testament prophecies, about the kingdom of Israel which Jesus in all the glory of his resurrection had the power to restore. Again, even when he was just about to leave them, Jesus did not answer their question directly. He simply said that it was not their concern. 'It is not for you to know times or seasons which the Father has fixed by his own authority. But you shall receive power when the Holy Spirit has come upon you; and you shall be my witnesses.' The new Kingdom is entrusted to them, even though they hardly know what kind of kingdom it is! And Jesus was taken from them. And while they were gazing into heaven as he went 'two men stood by them in white robes and said, "Men of Galilee, why do you stand looking into heaven? This Jesus, who was taken up from you into heaven, will come in the same way as you saw him go into heaven." [2]

Of course the final words 'he will come' must have made a deep impression on the apostles, who interpreted it as meaning he will come very soon, in a few days perhaps, or a few years. Perhaps they even thought that at this time of his return Jesus would at last restore the kingdom of Israel. But the reality was to be very different, and slowly the apostles became accustomed to it. Probably they discovered more during the years they lived after Jesus had left them than they had during the years they were with him.

[1]Acts 1:6
[2]Acts 1:11

29

They came to know him better. Jesus had told them: 'It is good for you that I am going away', as if his human presence, even while it revealed the Father, was at the same time an obstacle to this revelation, because he seemed so entirely human. And this obstacle still exists: for many people today Jesus of Nazareth is just a man.

Different and yet the same

In the accounts of Jesus' appearances after his resurrection, it is clear that Jesus is no longer living with the apostles; he appears to them and his appearances are rare and short. Jesus in his new state could not be visible to human eyes. The apostles of course recognized him, but somehow indirectly. Something had changed about him. Do you remember the story of the road to Emmaus: Jesus had blinded them so that they saw him without recognizing him? After some of the appearances the apostles had doubts and felt disturbed. To give them confidence Jesus showed them his wounds: 'See my hands and my feet, that it is I myself; handle me, and see; for a spirit has not flesh and bones as you see that I have.'[3] But there is still something different about these appearances. In an appearance reported by John, when the apostles were fishing in the Lake of Galilee, as they used to when Jesus was with them, because they needed to eat, Jesus stood on the shore and called them to ask if they had caught any fish. John says that the disciples did not recognize him. It was only after the miraculous catch that John said to Simon Peter: 'It is the Lord!'[4] And once they had landed 'none of the disciples dared ask him, "Who are you?" They knew it was the Lord.' We feel that there was something different about this recognition. Their relationship with their Master is not the same as it was during his earthly life, before his Passion and death.

[3]Lk. 24:39
[4]Jn. 21:1–12

What is meant by 'men in white robes' who spoke to the apostles after the Lord had gone up about 'this Jesus who was taken from you up into heaven'?[5] He has been taken away, so he will no longer be seen on earth by men, he has gone. Christ has passed into a different state and is somewhere else. This is what Jesus is trying to make the apostles understand by his new intermittent way of being with them, present but different, yet still the same Jesus. He is still the same person, the Messiah, the Saviour.

No doubt some of the apostles remembered the words Jesus had uttered in a moment of stress in which he told them of his fear of approaching death and how he longed to be glorified with the glory that was with his Father since before the creation.[6] It is rare to find in the Gospel words spoken by Jesus himself which sound as if they were spoken by the Word of God, the eternal Word of the Father. Jesus speaks as a man, and yet he speaks as the Word which is God.[7] 'The glory which I had with thee before the world was made.' These words contain the whole scope of Christ's self-awareness. He knows he is God, but his humanity is still painful and subject to fear because he must suffer death.

So what is this glory Jesus speaks of? It is not the mysterious and visible radiance which was revealed on Mount Tabor in his earthly human condition. God's glory is what makes God possess fully everything that we lack. It is God's Eternity, Goodness, Holiness, Greatness, God who is Love, God who is Truth. This is the fullness of the glory of God who is Life itself, that is why he is deathless. God's glory revealed beyond himself transforms those it touches to make them like God. Jesus is God but he is living an earthly life, just like ours.

Jesus took Peter, James and John, his closest companions, with him to the mountain to be witnesses of his

---

[5]Acts 1:10–11
[6]'Now Father, glorify thou me in thy presence with the glory which I had with thee before the world was made.' Jn. 17:5
[7]'Truly, truly, I say to you, before Abraham was, I am.' Jn. 8:58

31

'transfiguration'. The Gospel describes what happened: 'He was transfigured before them, and his garments became glistening, intensely white, as no fuller on earth could bleach them.'[8] The apostles were overwhelmed but at the same time they felt happy. They wanted this state to continue and to stay there with him. They hardly noticed that the transfigured Jesus was talking to Moses and Elijah about his coming death. This was like a twofold revelation of the Old Covenant with Moses and Elijah and the announcing of the death which was to seal the New Covenant, already accompanied by the glory which would follow it. The apostles could have learnt much from this if they had been in a state to understand the deep significance of what they were seeing.

These three apostles were also the ones who were with Jesus in his agony in the Garden of Gethsemane. They had glimpsed a sign of God's glory because this was not God's true glory which is invisible, but merely a sign of it bearable by human eyes and human understanding. In Gethsemane they needed no sign: Jesus spoke the language of human weakness, of pain and the sweat of blood. Here in the dark garden, as well as at the transfiguration and in Jesus' appearances after he had risen, the glory of God's life as it truly is was invisible. Then by his resurrection Christ was transformed by God's glory so that even as a man he was not usually visible. When Christ knocked Saul down on the road to Damascus, he also appeared in all the power of his glory. Saul fell to the ground, dazzled, and was changed in the very depths of his heart.

What is our hope?

'All authority in heaven and on earth has been given to me,' Jesus said.[9] All authority. That means the Creator's!

[8]Mk. 9:3
[9]Matt. 28:18

But still there are contradictions we do not understand. Yes, Jesus is the same and yet not still the same. He is still a man but he is not still a man subject to human laws, if we may thus express it. He is no longer in the same state as a dweller on earth. How can God's glory be compatible with Christ's humanity? This is what is puzzling. It seems so strange, so extraordinary, that it is barely acceptable to human reason. Nowadays people, even Christians, feel uncomfortable about this transformation of Christ after his death! Of course we are 'disciples' of Jesus, we read and meditate on the Gospel, we want to practise his teachings, especially about brotherly love. In his passion we see the greatest proof of love he could have given, as well as the redemption of all injustices because he himself was the victim of evil. But what about after his death? Yes, he has given us hope. But hope of what? The answer to this question is vague and we are hesitant in our thinking about what it actually means to say that Christ is alive now. This would presuppose a strong faith in a living God, the same faith as the apostles had from their Jewish tradition, the faith of Israel and Moses.

This is the true mystery and the centre of the christian faith, and it is this central mystery from which we sometimes draw back. Yes, indeed we do. Faith in the living God implies so many other things. Especially because the historical person of Christ seems explicable without having to refer to God. We have only to look at his human life, as it is reported to us, putting in brackets as part of the religious mentality of the first disciples the extraordinary miracles and the appearance of the risen Lord. When we do this we are left with the figure of a great prophet, a wise man who was the perfect example of a peaceful person, the innocent unjustly condemned. He is the embodiment of the ideal man. But is he God? Is he really still alive? And if he is why does he never show himself? He told his disciples that he would come back to take them with him. But now centuries have passed. The early Christians were at first enthusiastic in their expectation of his return, but then they seem to have grown tired of waiting. The first christian communities were clearly sustained by this hope of Christ's return, which helped them to live in a state of complete detachment from a world which would end so quickly. He had told them he would come like a thief in the night. And nothing happened. Indeed, the Son of man will return when he is no longer expected. He will knock at the door unexpectedly. But now two thousand years have passed. How can we still hope after such a long wait?

We only have experience of our own world, which is measurable by us. We have no direct experience of Christ and we cannot have. By this I do not mean that, like so many other Christians, and of course the saints, you have not occasionally had a certain experience of union with him. But you know very well that this experience is incommunicable and that people who try to analyse the human unconscious more or less scientifically are inclined to attribute a purely subjective value to such experiences. Such dreams will never alter the course of human history. We are enclosed within the confines of our own experience: experimental sciences, the exploration of the universe in all its dimensions from the most minute to the most vast, continually increase the sum of human knowledge. But nowhere do we find God, or Christ. This is the strongest way of emphasizing the supra-rational, or even anti-rational—as some think—nature of our simple statement that Christ is God, that he has risen from the dead and is alive in the fullness of life!

However, Christ's life now and the reality of a living God are not the only mysteries impenetrable to reason. There is the eternal problem of human self-awareness, the 'I' in each person. There is no need for me to tell you the extent to which we are a problem to ourselves our whole lives long: our need to love, our need to be loved, our suffering and weakness and then death which comes for us as it does for others. If we do not see these problems clearly in ourselves, we are constantly brought up against them in others. Whether we like it or not, there is an unanswerable

34

question in the nature of human self-awareness, and this question gives rise to the possibility of the existence of an Other, Another who is God. Faith introduces us to the answer to this question.

'He came from God'

The problems of preaching the Gospel to the modern world, which are obvious, are really problems which have always existed. But they are particularly difficult today because we live in a world which tries to do without a religious dimension. I mean the world of science and ideologies, not the world of personal needs and the dissatisfaction felt by seekers for the truth. Let us face the question squarely: Who is Jesus now? Where is the risen Christ? Has God got a universe? Scripture tells us: 'Man shall not see God and live'.[10] These are mysterious words! Does it mean that in human life as we know it, in our earthly state in which our minds work through our senses, no one can see God or know God directly? God is the inaccessible. Who has ever seen God? This is what gives force to Christ's words when he says he knows what he is talking about, and he alone knows, because he has come from God.[11] No man can see God and live. We should understand this death in several ways. It does not just mean that after death we will be able to see God, but also that there is an impassable barrier between God and us. For how could the mere fact of dying make us able to see God?

However, we believe that God made us for himself. What other reason could he have had for creating the human race? For it to find an end in itself? This does not make sense, even if we cease to be aware of the fact, even if we pretend to have accepted our mortality, we refuse death. I am not saying that most people have a conscious, explicit

[10]Ex. 33:20
[11]Jn. 8:13–19

35

desire for eternal life—that is not the same thing. Perhaps we feel the desire for it at certain moments. But still we cannot accept death. We hang on to life!

'You will follow me later'

I do not know whether you find it easy to long for what is called heaven. We must admit that there are times when it is hard to imagine this heaven. It is not even 'desirable'. If people are afraid of death, refuse to die, how is it that the idea of a life beyond, another life, fails to interest them or concern them? But this lack of interest about what might exist beyond the grave is quite natural. We can only be interested in life as we know it and care for it. This is a properly human life, with things to see, people to talk to and get to know. It is a social life and, above all, a life of feelings and love which we cannot imagine without our bodies and outside the world accessible to our senses. How could we want a different life? Is not losing this life losing everything? We can barely imagine a life in which there would be nothing to see, nothing to hear, no bodily feelings. That is why in centuries when faith was strong but simple, heaven was represented as a sort of earthly paradise, because people cannot conceive of happiness in any other way. We are made for life on earth.

Most people imagine this life after death as a place where they will meet again people they have loved. But how will we be able to meet them again? A woman who had suddenly lost her husband told me recently: 'I can't go to the cemetery yet, because I think of him as under the earth and I can't bear it.' What can we imagine about a reality that bears no relation to our present life?

The only reality that links us to this other world is a person: Jesus. When we think about it, it is an extraordinary thing, that a man should have been transfigured by God's glory. He is a whole universe, all by himself. Perhaps we accept this without difficulty, through force of habit.

We think of Jesus' transfiguration. But the reality is quite different. 'You will seek me and . . . where I am going you cannot come . . . where I am going you cannot follow me now but you shall follow me afterwards . . . I go to prepare a place for you.'[12] We cannot go where Jesus is without a radical transformation of our lives and our deepest selves, a transformation which is literally a rebirth.

'The Spirit gives life'

We must therefore speak of this new way of being of Christ's because our inner life, our ability to reach God in prayer and to be with Christ derives from it. This new mode of being of Christ's is also the way in which he is present in the Church and the Eucharist.

The first thing Jesus wants to make his apostles understand is that after his glorification, he is still the same Jesus as before, that he is still a man, but a man who is the Son of God, who is with God, his Father. As I have said it is hard to make sense of this. There is the continuity of the humanity of Christ, the continuity of the same person. 'It is I myself', as he said to his bewildered apostles.

For my part I cannot take lightly, as some exegetes seem to, the fact that the tomb was found empty. This is a sign Jesus gives us of the continuity of his humanity, his personal self, because he denies that he is a ghost:[13] 'See my hands and my feet, that it is I myself, handle me, and see; for a spirit has not flesh and bones as you see that I have.'[14] He asks for some fish and a little honey to eat to show the incredulous and amazed apostles that he is not a spirit. However, we repeat, he is not, he is no longer, the same Jesus as before, because what he has become the apostles are unable to contemplate. That is why these are appear-

[12] Jn. 13:32–14:3
[13] We should recall that, according to a very ancient tradition and the most generally held theological opinion, Christ's body was incorruptible.
[14] Lk. 24:39

ances which show Jesus risen and glorified, so that he is now invisible to people on earth. In the light of this we should re-read John chapter 6 where Jesus speaks of giving his body to eat. He even offers his 'flesh' as food and his 'blood' for us to drink. In the earthly state Christ was when he spoke these words, they were disgusting! And we can understand why the Jews were revolted. 'This is a hard saying. Who can listen to it?'[15] But Jesus is already thinking of himself in the state when his humanity will be transformed by God's glory and will be flesh without being flesh, blood without being blood. That is why he adds: 'It is the spirit that gives life, the flesh is of no avail.'[16] Herein lies the mystery of Christ's glorification, the mystery of humanity that remains humanity, but a humanity belonging to a God. Yes, we must realize how irrational and unbelievable such statements are, to have any idea of the leap in the dark faith requires of the unbeliever!

It is not easy to believe in Christ as God, but this is the essential, this is the heart of christian faith. Without this mystery our faith is nothing. The repercussions of this faith are what should make all Christians, wherever they are, and whatever they do, a true 'yeast' in the human dough.

He comes to meet us

We say: God is hidden. God is not visible. God does not show himself. As if we were reproaching him. No, God is simply God. God does not hide, but he cannot be seen, which is a different matter. We are not in a fit state to see him, or even to see Christ in his present state, but still the almighty power that has been given him over heaven and earth enables him to reign in our hearts. This is the dark mysterious meeting place, where love is able to overcome the divine barrier. But Christ wanted to show himself to

[15]Jn. 6:60
[16]Jn. 6:63

the apostles in such a way that they could believe that he was alive and glorified, and he comes to us too, through certain signs that faith can recognize. First and above all, there is the witness and the faith of the apostles. They were what Jesus wanted them to be. 'You shall be my witnesses.'[17] And from witness to witness we go back to the faith of the apostles themselves in the person of Jesus, his divine person, the presence of Christ glorified, Son of God, the eternal Son of the Father.

We should constantly strive to become more aware of this faith, to kindle it in our hearts and in that of every disciple who is God's dwelling place, a temple of the Spirit and a member of the Body of Christ. We must also kindle our faith in Christ's presence in the Church, the Eucharist, and also in the other sacraments, of which the Eucharist is the centre and the source.

But we should not try to imagine some sort of presence to our senses. Presence is essentially a relationship, a real live relationship between two people, so that each is attentive to the other and knows that the other is also attentive to him. Christ is present to me because I know he is looking at me deep into the depths of my thoughts. I know that he knows me and listens to me. I also believe that he is capable of working all-powerfully in my life and in the lives of all his other human brothers. There is nothing wrong in our imagining this presence of God's Son as a human presence, and usually we cannot do otherwise. We do not pretend to be angels, we are earthly beings. Jesus appeared to his apostles to confirm them in their faith and hope, and even if these appearances were not as he really was, they were still authentic and true because of what they signified of an invisible reality.

This problem of Christ as God is a problem for all mankind, today more than ever. In Christ we have the very mystery of the person, the mystery of every human person. In his Church, he is also the source of communion

[17] Acts 1:8

and love in the unity of his Body. There seems to be a contradiction between notions of human collectivity, an organized crowd and the idea of a personal life and destiny. This problem is more acute than it ever was. The human race has multiplied by thousands of millions and risks losing the sense of individual importance and dignity. Respect for the sacred unique character of each person and his living-space is in grave danger.

Once again, I invite you at the end of this chapter to recall the thinking of the apostle John, and to re-read his accounts of the appearances of the risen Christ, to renew your faith in the living, eternally living and divine person of Christ.

IV

Glorification of the Son of Man

The mystery of Christ glorified is at the centre of our faith, our life as Christians, and especially if that life is consecrated to God. We should be aware of the effect this mystery should have on our personal lives, and also on mankind as a whole in the world today.

We often find that Christians nowadays feel troubled or shaken in their faith, because with our current scientific mentality we need to find a new expression of our faith to suit our changed situation. It is not easy for Christians today to believe simply that the risen Jesus is alive and glorified, that one day we shall meet him, that he is the centre of a universe called heaven or eternal life. We have to understand what this means. Which of us can imagine or even express to ourselves in comprehensible, and thus communicable, language what God is and what the divine condition of a human being could be like? Jesus was in an earthly condition like ours. So we can understand Jesus as the Son of man, his love for us, expressed by feelings, words, actions and the sacrifice of his life. We can understand Christ's sufferings, his agony and abandonment, his death. But we cannot understand his glory, his risen state.

We know the human condition only too well. Human sciences struggle to understand it in all its various aspects, the biological, the sociological, the psychological, the spiritual. Our bodies have an animal life, a life of the senses, and we know how weighed down our spiritual lives can be, even at our highest moments, by our animal condition, and it always remains entirely dependent on our senses. If God is a spirit, he remains invisible; if he is alive, his life is quite different from our bodily lives.

In the present climate this question is all the more puzzling because we find it difficult to conceive of a world that is not material, because for most of our contemporaries, what is not material is nothing, it is not real. During the early centuries there was always speculation in the Church on this opposition between the bodily and the spiritual, whether the problem was the resurrection of Jesus, his transfiguration, the mystery of his being both the God of glory and the man suffering and dying, the relation between his glorious risen body and earthly bodies on earth.

Sharing the divine state

We find signs of these applications in the epistles of the apostle Paul, when he considers the human situation. We could even suspect him of a kind of dualism. His letters frequently show a struggle in his deepest self between flesh and spirit,[1] between the old man and the new.[2] However, this awareness, which comes from his own experience, does not make him despise the body. For him the Christian's body is God's temple.[3] Christ must be glorified in our bodies.[4] He also speaks of the transformation of our lowly bodies into glorious bodies.[5] That is why we must offer our bodies as living sacrifices.[6] However, Paul finds this fleshly

[1]'For the desires of the flesh are against the Spirit, and the desires of the Spirit are against the flesh; for these are opposed to each other, to prevent you from doing what you would.' Gal. 5:17
[2]Eph. 4:22; Col. 3:9
[3]1 Cor. 3:16; 'Do you not know that your body is a temple of the Holy Spirit. . . .' 1 Cor. 6:19
[4]'So glorify God in your body.' 1 Cor. 6:20
[5]'The Lord Jesus Christ, who will change our lowly body to be like his glorious body. . . .' Phil. 3:21
[6]Rom. 12:1

body a heavy weight: it prevents him from seeing Christ. Remaining in this body means living in exile, far from the Lord.[7] 'Who will deliver me from the body of this death?'[8]

Our contemporaries find such language hard to understand.[9] What can be the sense in an object of faith which is such an inconceivable reality as the transformation of Christ's human nature, so that it is no longer material but spiritual? What is this human nature which is no longer human nature? How can human nature share the divine? Human reason asks these questions. Hence the tendency to think of this expression of the christian faith as more or less mythological, and that the Gospel should be interpreted to mean that humanity survives death in some way without being very precise about how. If we are to believe in Christ in glory, the christian hope, the resurrection of the body, must we keep a childish credulity, and refuse to question our faith with our minds, our sciences, our knowledge gained from experience? We no longer live in a religious-minded world. Nevertheless the purpose of human life, the reality of the invisible dimension of mankind as Christ's body, mankind redeemed by Christ, the existence of Christ himself, in person, as the first man to be glorified, this whole christian universe, can only be accepted through faith: it must be believed by faith and cannot be proved by reason.

Through our consecration we live in a religious universe. We should not be afraid of admitting it. The way we look at our brotherhood, our lives, the Church, the world and

[7] 'We know that while we are at home in the body we are away from the Lord . . . we would rather be away from the body and at home with the Lord.' II Cor. 5:6,8
[8] 'We groan inwardly as we wait for adoption as sons, the redemption of our bodies.' Rom. 8:23
[9] Even materialists do not deny the existence and value of the human mind and spiritual life: but for them these are manifestations of human life, with no real distinction between matter and spirit, as two different orders of being. Such a division has no meaning for them; they are interested in experimental analysis of manifestations of human life, which is thought of, observed and studied as one indivisible reality.

43

its development, the political problems that trouble it, and its many moral problems, must be a way of seeing things that is a constant effort—even though we may sometimes fail through clumsiness or narrowness—to translate Christ's Gospel into human realities. We must try to see things as Jesus does. Yes, the world of faith does exist, and it is a real world: it is the property of faith to carry with it the conviction, which is like a clear insight, establishing the reality of what is believed in.

Are there many who live at the level of this Christ's world? The religious world is being pushed out further and further by the political world, the scientific and technical world, which gives no importance to a religious universe, or at any rate no scientific value. This seems obvious to many people. And if we try to say what we mean by Christ glorified, do not we run into many contradictions? Of course we say, as the angel of the Lord said to Mary: 'With God nothing is impossible.' But still, human reason mutters, no, it is not possible!

The sacrament of unity

However, the political world with which the religious world mingles, still has certain islands of religious feeling. I do not mean people who have faith, and there are some in every religion, I do not mean believing and generous Christians, I mean a sociological factor, the existence of a religious mentality. It is a bit like the hot and cold air currents which are both in the atmosphere but do not mix. There are still relics of a religious world existing side by side with the political world, whose only horizon is history, this world's history, the history of mankind. Some believers in Christ try to find a meaning for their faith in this context and to work out the repercussions of the mystery of Christ in terms of this history. These repercussions are the only conceivable object, the only conceptual content that can be given to faith which makes sense to political reason, the only content that can be translated into specific generous action, a leaven of revolution for the transformation of the world. Is not this doing Christ's will? Is not it God's will that there should be Christ's plan for history? Yes, these are two ways of seeing the world, two perspectives. Can the one be separated from the other? Should we accept the existence of two opposing types of Christian? Can the religious man not accept this historical vision of the redemption of mankind in its political and even its ideological implications? And can those who are completely involved in the work of transforming the world attach any importance to a religious view of the universe, especially when this view seems incapable on its own of changing the world?

At the centre of this universe stands Christ glorious. Is not he the great and wholly new reality St Paul speaks of? We must take this faith in Christ as God to its logical conclusions. If we take the Gospel as it is—and not as it is interpreted by some people—if we analyse objectively the content of its message we discover that it does have a double perspective. Is the aim of the Gospel, Jesus' message, to make God man's centre? Or is its aim to reveal to man his own true dignity? We claim that these two interpretations are interdependent and not contradictory. This gives us two interpretations of the Gospel corresponding to the two kinds of Christians we have been talking about. Yes, God reveals himself, God the Father reveals himself in Jesus, and Jesus must be worshipped as God. We worship him as God, as the eternal Son of the Father, and the Christian becomes first and foremost, not only the servant but also the son of the Father, that is a 'man for God', because man is for God's glory. We exist for God's glory, the glory of the Holy Trinity. In this light the Eucharist must be seen as man's sacrifice, the sacrifice of the Son of God, a sacrifice of adoration, praise, reparation and thanksgiving.

Others, on the other hand, will see Jesus' humanity as the revelation of man's greatness and freedom, which no one else has manifested as fully as the Son of man, Jesus,

45

the most perfect of men, the most free, the most aware and the most loving. Then we can say that man is God's glory. And it is true. And Christ is the glory of man. In this light the Eucharist is seen first and foremost as food, spiritual bread, a divine food to help man learn to live lovingly. It is the sacrament of unity, of the community of brothers gathered together by Christ.

It is a good thing to remind ourselves of these two ways of looking at the Sacrament of the Lord. Sometimes it is not merely a difference of emphasis. In fact there are two kinds of spirituality, two attitudes to Christ's mystery and his sacrament.

The way of love

Now we should speak briefly about the repercussions the risen Christ's glory, the glory of the Father himself, should have on human relationships. What are the repercussions of God's revelation in Christ? Jesus said that he was Truth and Light. He said that God was Love, absolute Love and Life. Light and truth concern both our self-awareness and our conception of mankind's destiny. Does Christ really throw light on this destiny? By talking about love and life, does Jesus bring anything new? Or is it just a question of making people aware of the quality of love already rooted in them, which they could tend and make grow by themselves? Are we or are we not left to our own devices? Of course the answer is not as black or white as this. However, the way some people see the reign of the Spirit in history and in men's hearts as independent of God's revelation in Christianity, might make us ask whether Jesus' coming was really necessary, whether he brought anything really 'new' to the relationship between God and man.

Yes, we should love God by loving our brothers, loving other people, loving mankind. We should love as sons of God and love God's Son by loving men. Both John and Paul show us the close link between these two loves. We

46

have spoken of the invisibility and even inconceivability of the godhead of a God that no one has ever seen,[10] that no one on earth has ever been able to look at. But the way of love, and only the way of love, can lead to a genuine meeting between man and God. All the saints have experienced such a meeting and the Gospel tells us so.[11] But did it matter or not in this meeting, that God, by revealing himself through his Son, Jesus Christ, revealed a love whose depth can only be sounded by confessing Christ's godhead, a love which we know is able to transfigure us into God, sons of God? In a word, was Christ's coming necessary to teach us how to love our brothers to the full?

We know from our own experience, before we even consider that of others, that self-fulfilment requires a meeting, an encounter with another, others, an Other who is God. Most people do not experience an encounter with God except through their encounter with others. Jesus tells us we must 'lose our life'[12] for his sake. We must also lose ourselves for others, we must make ourselves available and also open our minds to understand the other person. We need the insight to be able to put ourselves in other people's places, or as Jesus puts it very simply: 'Whatever you wish that men would do to you, do so to them; for this is the law and the prophets.'[13] It sounds so simple but it is very difficult to do!

Jesus says that anything we do to the least of his brothers we do to him, and what we fail to do for them we fail to do for him. We can take these words in two ways: we can either say that God asks us only to serve other people, do good to them, without it being necessary to think about God, because what we do to or for others we do to or for God. We can also say that we cannot learn how to serve

[10]'No one has ever seen God; the only Son who is in the bosom of the Father, he has made him known.' Jn. 1:18
[11]'You shall love the Lord your God.' Matt. 22:37; 'He who does not love does not know God; for God is love.' 1 Jn. 4:8
[12]Matt. 10:39, 16:25
[13]Matt. 7:12

47

other people well if we do not know Christ's love for us and love him in return. It is true that not everyone is able to know Christ and yet God goes out to meet everyone. The secret road of each of these people towards his or her perfection, destiny, through a lifetime's struggle is a secret known to God alone.

But we must also reckon with an event outside man's scope, the incarnation of the Word, which is an event in the historical sense and also outside history. Jesus, God's Word, and all he revealed during his short life on earth and how he is in glory, is connected, of course, with humanity, and is also a mystery we must try to understand, go deeper into and live by. And we cannot live by it if it is not proclaimed to us by men who were witnesses of it. Otherwise there would be no mission, no Church. Jesus would not have needed a Church if he had not decided to build everything on these witnesses he had chosen. But the question remains whether we can do without Christ, in the work of perfecting human society and in learning to love fully.

Is it possible fully to love the poorest or the least lovable of men without reference to Christ, Christ disfigured by his Passion and now in glory? Without Christ could we care for one another, for the poor, with a truly great love? This is not an easy question to answer. It amounts to asking whether mankind is capable of reaching a certain degree of perfection and justice in society without Christ? Or can this perfection only come with Christ? Because we also know from experience that the Lord's disciples are not always those who have learnt to love best, are not necessarily those best able to translate this love into effective and just action. We often meet people who do not know the Lord who teach us important lessons in love, in justice and generosity. When I say that these people do not know the Lord, I do not mean that the light of the Spirit of God has not touched their hearts, I mean that they have not met Christ in faith. Even if we suppose that Christ's death and resurrection made a reconciliation between mankind and

God, and that with this reconciliation the reign of the Spirit in Christ's name began, the question still remains: was it necessary for Christ to be known and acknowledged as Son of God by men, and is it necessary to his reign today that he should be known and acknowledged as Son of God by our contemporaries?

The leaven is not for itself

This is why I want to try to place—just that—Christ's role in the political history of mankind. I mean particularly Christ's effect on your individual lives. We have spoken of human relationships and we know that no one can become fully himself without relationships with others. You cannot be genuinely Christian unless you work to create a community of brothers with good relationships between the members. You are members of one another and every Church community is the Body of Christ. We must not forget this. Politics are concerned with some part, but only some part, of human relationships. It has rightly been said that the world today, given its complexity, condemns people to depend in nearly every aspect of their lives on the political order. We see this in every type of political order actually in existence. However, it is still true that in most cases, the political order only concerns certain human relationships indirectly. The daily life of a child, for example, its upbringing, its family, the love between its parents, depends very indirectly on the political order, even if by political order we mean decent housing, working and living conditions. However, when these conditions necessary to a decent life are fulfilled, everything else is on the level of love. I would even say that the better the material conditions, the more acute the problem of love.

Love is not simply doing works of justice. The thirst for peace, the need to be at peace with oneself and family, the people we are in daily contact with, the blossoming of the life of the spirit and other essential needs will always be there, and the political order cannot satisfy them. Never mind other questions such as suffering, illness, ageing and death. And I am not even speaking of people who are deprived or handicapped in all sorts of ways so that for them life has lost all meaning if it is not of divine origin and does not have a future with God.

We know that we are made for a mutual interdependence of service and communion—by God's will, by our human nature itself, and also because Christ's first commandment is to love. The Church when it speaks most genuinely with Christ's voice should constantly remind us of this, and every genuine christian life should be a daily effort to accomplish this.

Yes, as the apostle Paul says, we are members of one another. That is why the lack of unity and refusal of communion are deep wounds in Christ's own Body. And when I speak of Christ's Body, I take Paul's expression seriously, because for Paul this is not a symbol but the reality of Christ's humanity in its divine condition which enables him to be all in all. If Christ's revelation of man's dignity is true, if man is God's son, destined for eternal life, and his human nature however weak and wretched is destined to be glorified, this means that love should look at other people, especially the most deprived, differently. But when we proclaim these facts of Christ's glory, the unity of all people in Christ and the destiny of divine transfiguration of our human nature for every one of us, we are saying things that are simply unbelievable by most reasonable people and those who do not have a religious frame of mind. If we try to avoid this difficulty by interpreting the faith, by reducing it to the effects of Christ's mystery on the world, our faith becomes weak, blind and cannot see the light. That is why when Jesus speaks of the things of the Kingdom of God among men, he uses a language we can never quite grasp because he is speaking of a reality which it is very difficult to define.

Jesus has a reason for comparing the Kingdom of God to leaven, that is to say a mysterious reality whose purpose

50

is not for itself, for leaven is not for itself—if it is not put in the dough it goes bad. For it to work it must be well mixed in the dough. Jesus knew what he was talking about when he used this simile.

This is the destiny of christian faith among mankind. Christians are active everywhere, but everywhere they are people just like other people, and they will always be faced with the problem of their faith. Their faith is like sap circulating in the vine. This sap can give life to everything, and energy to every human plan. But it is only sap, it does not of itself create human plans. And as we are speaking of political projects, different social systems, it is up to human reason to construct these with the help of human intelligence and the human sciences. As for people who have faith in God, who are disciples of Christ, they are enlivened by the sap of the Gospel in all their activities.

To the making and carrying out of their plans, Christians bring the sap of the Gospel and the leaven of Christ. That is why Christians have no specifically christian political programme, but they are always in a difficult situation, because they cannot allow the sap of the Gospel to dry up at its source which is Christ God, or the leaven to go bad because it has lost its divine power. Because the sap can be cut off from its source and the leaven can lose its power if it is separated from Christ. When Christ is no longer referred to, when the christian body is not attached to Christ, then there is a cut-off, one could say a sociological cut-off, the rejection of Christ through a materialist view of the world.

Faith and effectiveness on earth

I know that in these two interpenetrating universes, the religious and the political, there are some things the Christian can never surrender, and he must be prepared to die for his faith, even if it does not seem very important for the future of human society. He must be convinced, even if

51

appearances are to the contrary, that his faith is a treasure for the world. But we cannot prove it. That is why the Christian as a Christian is often a poor sort of man. He is clumsy in expressing his faith, and as a believer he is not always among the most effective workers for the world's good.

Maritain remarked that in the course of history certain christian values, such as peace, justice, brotherhood have been taken up by unbelievers or materialists, or even anti-Christians, and through them these gospel values gave rise to sociologically effective projects, which Christians had been unable to construct. We also know that there is a kind of effectiveness which the Christian cannot allow because he feels he has not the right to use certain means opposed to his view of humanity. But how long can these christian values keep their force and purity if they are cut off from their source? Moreover, not all Christians behave well. Perhaps they do not understand their faith very well, perhaps they are paralysed by a narrow vision, because their love is lukewarm, or perhaps they have not the talents necessary to help transform society. But they still want to be sincere disciples of the Lord!

This makes us wonder whether there is not a division of labour in historical reality. There is the mission of some to preserve the leaven of faith in Christ in its purity and to bear witness to the light Christ throws on human destiny. These Christians, especially the members of religious orders among them, see people in the light of the Gospel, and respect them all for Christ's sake, and perhaps this makes them incapable of participating in certain revolutionary works which can only be brought about by sacrificing certain gospel values, by repression of freedom and treating men collectively. Because of the means employed in such revolutionary action, Christians will not necessarily be the most effective in bringing about changes; they have noticed a certain quality of tenderness in Christ for the poorest, his mercy for sinners, the most despised in society, they have discovered in Christ the freedom of faith and hope, they have chosen to live among the most deprived, the least of Christ's brothers, the only ones to whom he promised to reveal himself completely. I think only God knows who is the most effective. However, for people in religious orders there is a choice to be made: there are some things which cannot be done without sacrificing other relative values.

V

The Reign of Christ's Spirit and the Leaven of History

'As yet the Spirit had not been given because Jesus was not yet glorified.'[1] These words of John the Evangelist are important. He does not mean only that the reign of the Spirit began after the ascension of Jesus as a result and fulfilment of his work, but that by his glorification, the humanity of the God-Man passed into a state in which Christ could reign over human hearts in a mysterious way and in total communion with the Spirit sent by his Father. When Jesus acts the Father acts as well as the Holy Spirit. A totally new reality was revealed in the hearts of the disciples after Christ's glorification, because this glorification made the human Jesus capable of working in the same way as the divine Spirit. Did not Jesus give a glimpse of this at the end of his speech on the bread of life? His conclusion was: 'It is the spirit that gives life, the flesh is of no avail.'[2] Nevertheless, without this transfigured flesh there would be no reign of the Spirit such as there is in the Church.

We have spoken of Jesus' glorification. Now we must talk about the reign of his Spirit.

[1] Jn. 7:39
[2] Jn. 6:63

The Spirit and the mystery of Jesus

Lately both inside and outside the Church there has been a renewal of spontaneous prayer which is attributed to the Holy Spirit. It is as if the active presence of the Spirit of God had been discovered. This movement is developing side by side with a genuine cult of the Word of God. All this has had an effect on Christians, breaking down their old habits of expression in their prayers, as well as certain preconceptions about the practice of their religion. It has also caused some confusion. If we were to believe some people, up till now the Holy Spirit has been forgotten about altogether! There are others who are always talking about the Holy Spirit without laying themselves open to his action. There are others still who hardly ever talk about the Holy Spirit and yet humbly let themselves be effectively guided by him.

I think that our times are like all others, in that there is always renewal in the Church, which is subject to constant renewal because this is the law of all spiritual life. The Church is in constant need of renewal because the weight of human limitations tends to drag it down into mediocrity and routine. It needs continual renewal movements which are attributed to the Holy Spirit. Is it not a bit childish to think there is something special about the time we live in? But people at all times have felt this about their own time.

No doubt some of you learnt in your catechism as children that the centre of our faith is the mystery of the Trinity: Father, Son and Holy Spirit. Nowadays we do not hear very much about the Trinity. It is rare to hear God called by this name. People talk about the Spirit, the Word, Jesus, the Father. Perhaps you will say that this comes to the same thing—they are talking about the Trinity. Yes, this is true in one sense. But we get the impression that the idea of the divine unity of the three persons has been lost, that we no longer dare formulate this mystery of God's inner life. One single God acts: when the Spirit acts God acts; when the Word becomes incarnate in Jesus, God

55

becomes incarnate. It is never easy to try to reflect upon the mystery of the divine life. That is why we pass from one imperfect conception of it to another, even though we may have a true insight into the nature of divinity. For the truth of these realities is different from the truth of language.

Let us go back to the Gospel and Jesus' earthly life to see what the evangelists attribute to the Holy Spirit who is in fact ever present.

First, Jesus was conceived of the Holy Spirit in the womb of the Virgin Mary. There was no intervention of an earthly father. His conception is thus rightly attributed to the Holy Spirit. Then the Spirit is manifested in Jesus, the beloved Son, when he is baptized by John the Baptist. In comparing the baptism of John with the baptism of Jesus, the evangelist tells us that Jesus alone baptizes in the Spirit.[3] We are also told that when Jesus withdrew into the desert, he was driven by the Spirit.[4] It is the Spirit who appears to lead Jesus to the knowledge of his mission. This comes out in several passages in the Gospel. Jesus works in Galilee with the power of the Spirit[5] and he trembles with joy under the influence of the Spirit.[6] He drives out devils by the power of the Spirit.[7] Finally, when he tells his apostles what will happen after he has gone and what is to become of his teaching, he speaks of the Spirit of Truth, the Paraclete, the Comforter, who will enlighten and strengthen them. Jesus goes so far as to say that it is good for his disciples that he is going away, so that they can live by the power of the Holy Spirit.[8] He tells them that the Spirit will teach them all things, make them remember his teachings

[3]'He who sent me to baptize with water said to me, "He on whom you see the Spirit descend and remain, this is he who baptizes with the Holy Spirit," ' Jn. 1:33
[4]'Then Jesus was led up by the Spirit . . .' Matt. 4:1.; 'The Spirit immediately drove him out into the wilderness.' Mk. 1:12
[5]Lk. 4:14
[6]Lk. 10:21
[7]Matt. 12:28
[8]Jn. 16:7–15

and guide them into all Truth.[9] Before he leaves them Jesus bestows on them the Spirit with the power to forgive sins in God's name: 'Receive the Holy Spirit.'[10]

Perhaps we wonder why, if Jesus was God, did he need to be moved by the Spirit? What does this mean? We must not forget that Jesus was also fully human. He possessed a human nature. He had a human mind and a human heart. His humanity was truly like ours and like us he had a human consciousness. And it was at this level of his humanity that the Spirit enlightened him, drove him and led him. But the Spirit is not separate from the Word incarnate or from the Father who sent him. God acts in a way which makes us think that, although there are three persons in God, there is a single action. It is always God who acts in each of the three persons. God's action is attributed to the Spirit when it accompanies human beings to enlighten them, guide them and comfort them. Jesus in his human nature needed to be enlightened, guided and comforted by the Spirit, the Spirit of God, the Spirit of his Father, the Spirit of the One he himself was. The Spirit's working on Jesus was the echo at the level of his human faculties of the divine action which emanated from his very being as Son of God, for as long as his humanity remained in its earthly state, because after his death, when he was in glory, his whole human nature was in a different condition, as we have seen.

I sometimes get the impression that people nowadays have a tendency to speak of the Spirit as a sort of independent being, a sort of new deity. A kind of opposition is set up between our time and other times in the past, and now the reign of the Spirit has come. But it would be a great oversimplification to say that the Old Covenant was the Father's time, that there was a period which was the Son's time and now we are living in the time of the Spirit. It is

[9] Jn. 15:26; 14:26; 16:13
[10] Jn. 20:22

57

true in one sense that the Church's time is also the time of the reign of the Spirit.

But if we call our time the time of the Spirit, this is saying that Jesus is absent—and when I say absent, I mean the term in the meaning proper to the human state, that is to say that we can no longer see Jesus, or hear him or ask him questions or even feel his presence. But as we have said when we were talking about the divine state of his humanity, not just the Word, but the Word incarnate in Jesus, the Son in glory accompanies the work of the Spirit and the work of the Father. But Jesus in his divine condition is absent from us as an earthly man. So we should speak of this active and mysterious presence as God's reign, God's action. This is the Kingdom of God. I think we can say that the Kingdom of God and the reign of the Spirit are the same thing.

'I am with you always . . .'

So what is the nature of the action of the Spirit sent by Jesus?[11] This gives rise to many questions! With our limitations and our rational way of thinking about things, we always have a tendency to think of the action of the Holy Spirit in a human way, that is in a way we can picture to ourselves, and this has its disadvantages! The work of the Spirit is God's work, giving life to man, enlightening, advising and guiding him. God walks hand in hand with human freedom, of course without destroying it, but strengthening it. We could say that man's freedom is impregnated with the divine. This is the mystery, because it is always difficult to speak about the Holy Spirit; if we stress the responsibility of man, a responsibility which remains entirely his, it sounds as if we are minimizing the action of the Holy Spirit, by rationalizing man's behaviour left to his own devices. And if on the other hand we stress

[11]'And behold, I send the promise of my Father upon you.' Lk. 24:49

the freedom of the Spirit, it sounds as if we are saying that in certain cases man should deny the light of his reason and let himself be guided by another light. But which? How does this light of the Spirit show itself? What happens between God and us? Between Jesus in glory and us who feel like orphans left all alone? But Jesus promised that he would not leave us orphans.[12] And his last words were: 'Lo, I am with you always, to the close of the age.'[13]

But how can Jesus be with us? The action of the Holy Spirit, which accompanied Christ in his earthly condition, which was of course a different situation from ours, but still an earthly condition, accompanied him to the end, till the moment when he gave the apostles their mission and the descent of the Spirit at Pentecost. This descent was the solemn sign of the beginning of the reign of the Spirit, its inauguration. It was also the beginning of the life of the Church, the beginning of a new active, enlightening presence of Christ among his disciples, and even among all men. Because every man who is born into this world is enlightened by the Spirit of God[14] to the extent to which he is honest, open and humble.

So what do we mean by this emphasis on the Spirit at the present time, to the point where charismatic gifts directly attributed to the Spirit are considered completely new, as an invitation to go beyond our own reason and our own plans? And what do we mean by freedom in the Holy Spirit? Are we really more free? What is the nature of this freedom in the Spirit, freedom not to contradict the Spirit or to put ourselves in his place, but to let ourselves be guided by him? We hear about the inventions of the Spirit. Are they inventions of the Holy Spirit or inventions of men who ascribe them to the Spirit? Jesus in the Gospel tells us about the Spirit of Truth which will come to those who believe in him. When in the last chapter we were speaking

[12]'I will not leave you desolate; I will come to you.' Jn. 14:18
[13]Matt. 28:20
[14]Jn. 1:9

about the condition of Christ glorified in his humanity, we stressed the special position of the Christian, who is different from other people, not because of his qualities or even his generosity and charity, but because he believes, because he has given himself entirely to Christ by faith, because he has met Christ. The Christian believes, and this faith is a light of truth to him.[15]

No, I do not think that the Church or Christians have ever, in any age, forgotten the work of the Holy Spirit. Perhaps they just spoke about it differently. We cannot consider holiness in the Church without considering it a work of the Spirit. We have only to remember the long line of holy men and women who have illuminated the holiness of the Church or who began spiritual movements which many Christians followed. They are not a small élite, but spiritual movements, which began with certain individuals, precisely because of a special action of the Holy Spirit. These gifts have never been lacking in the christian community throughout its history. In the past, people spoke more than they do today about the seven gifts of the Spirit given to every Christian at baptism. The number seven was used to symbolize the fullness of the Spirit's action, and the baptized person was enabled to be guided and strengthened by the Spirit in the knowledge of God and the things of God by the light of truth. And this light was also thrown upon human realities, so that the Christian became capable of acting with Christ's wisdom and prudence. Every Christian has this capacity to be guided by the Spirit. But we must admit that certain ideas about the spiritual life, a narrowness of vision, a certain legalism and formalism were able in certain ages to suppress this capacity and these gifts which can only be active if the heart is alive with charity.

It is not easy to speak of these things, because every time we stress one aspect, we need to stress another equally. Why? Because in this sphere of the reign of the Spirit we

[15]Jn. 1:12

60

are at the meeting place of God's freedom with man's. It is the meeting point of God's plans and actions, with human plans, either at the personal level or the broader social level. What do we know about God's plans? Has God got plans? Can we know what they are? We already find it quite difficult enough to grasp God's plan in his work of redemption, liberation, through the cross of Christ and his resurrection! But when we try to grasp God's plan in the history of the world, then we risk making mistakes with dramatic consequences! If we asked Jesus about this would not he tell us what he told the apostles? 'It is not for you to know times or seasons which the Father has fixed by his own authority.'[16]

This Spirit who is a living person and a divine action is called the Spirit of God, the Spirit of holiness, because it is by this breath of God that man can progress towards holiness as a son of God. He is called the Spirit of love because he is the bond of love between the Father and Son in God, and also because his essential work in men's heart is the work of love. He is called the Spirit of adoption, the Spirit of Jesus, because he alone gives us the power to become children of God,[17] and only the Spirit can testify that we are sons of God[18], children of God. We cannot learn to behave as children of God without sharing the Spirit of sonship which God alone can give us in his Son. We are not only God's children because he made us, or because we are in God's image and we share in his self-awareness, freedom, intelligence and capacity to love; we are also sons in the deeper sense because now we are destined to share in the divine Sonship of God's only Son. Of course, this mystery requires great faith if it is to mean anything in our lives. What difference can we see between the human lives of those who believe they are truly God's

[16]Acts 1:7
[17]Jn. 1:12
[18]'. . . it is the Spirit himself bearing witness with our spirit that we are children of God.' Rom. 8:16; cf. Gal. 4:6

children, and those who simply behave freely and generously, without knowing that they are God's children?

The Spirit's freedom and man's responsibility

In order to clarify these thoughts, we should try to distinguish different levels of activity in human beings. There are not many people—are there any?—who feel united within themselves. We are divided against ourselves. These deep divisions are the cause of our sufferings, our anguish, the difficulties that we find in 'being ourselves', in fulfilling ourselves. Still there are different levels of action in us. Firstly we are faced with the world around us. We are told that God created man and put him in the Garden of Eden to cultivate it.[19] Man is also master over the different life forms and the animals. A whole view of man and his relationship to the universe underlies these primitive accounts in Genesis. Yes, man is the lord of the universe.

Modern man is becoming more and more aware of this situation, as his knowledge and technical capacities develop. This is his domain and he feels free and responsible for it. There is a properly human responsibility for the world, which is not taken away from man by the fact that he is invited by Jesus to share in the divine life as a human creature. Man is an earthly being by nature and he is left to his own devices in all that concerns the organization of his work, even the most primitive, as well as in the organization of his social life, from the patriarchal family, the tribe, to the most complex forms of industrial society. This is the history men themselves make. To what extent is this history accompanied by the Spirit of God, the Spirit of Jesus, the Lord of History? This is still the Father's secret.

Every man is accompanied by the Spirit of God, but we should not think of this as restricting his responsibilities.

[19]Gen. 1:26–31

Man is left to his own devices. That is why he is gifted with intelligence. God alone knows how his own sovereign freedom, a freedom which is full of love for this weak creature created by his breath, leads man without restricting him. The author of life cannot not respect each human creature which bears the image of the Trinity. God cannot fail to accompany him, but he does not interfere with man's freedom.

It is not for us to know—because no one can—the way in which God accompanies us. God himself created our consciousness and free will, so we cannot feel what he works in them. We are too inclined to seek the exceptional, to think that any action or impulse of God in us must be distinct from our own. This is a big mistake because it means that we only see the extraordinary, what can be attributed directly to God, as the action of the Spirit in human lives. We would like our lives to be sprinkled with miracles, miracles of light, miracles of self-transformation, miracles of liberation. Of course the Spirit is Another, and produces in us the desires and wishes of Another. But this Spirit is not a stranger, he does not make his action take the place of ours; on the contrary he allows us to be responsible and in charge of our lives. He makes us see, he makes us want, he makes us choose, but it is we who see, want and choose. The disciple of Jesus is dwelt in by Another, who is so close to him[20] that he makes him free, because this Spirit is God's own freedom in him, because God alone is wholly free.

We must accept our situation as creatures and our human condition in relationship with the material universe and our environment which is the society of our fellows. This huge totality of mankind, which is becoming ever more complex, dominates us, although it is we who have created it and who have the power to modify the relationships between individual members. The complexity of servitude and oppression in which we are now involved is one

[20]'It is no longer I who live, but Christ who lives in me.' Gal. 2:20

of the great problems of our time. And we wonder: in all this is man accompanied by the Spirit of God? Of course he is accompanied by the Spirit in that he has consciousness, freedom, intelligence and will. But if man weakens his freedom, if he allows his will to be enslaved by his passions, and if his intelligence is darkened by discursive reason or by pride, then he is left on his own, to his own decisions, because he has withdrawn himself, perhaps without knowing it, from the influence of the Spirit in him.

There is truth in the idea that man is master of himself and the universe. It is true that we cannot abdicate from the heavy responsibilities we bear for all that is happening in history, the violence, the injustice, the oppression. For who else is responsible? The Spirit? Are we borne along passively by blind destiny? Jesus said that without him we could do nothing![21] We should meditate on these words, because either their meaning is terrible or they contradict what we have just said. And since we are speaking of man's place in the universe and the relationship between him and the working of the Spirit of God, I should like to say a word about what is called 'history', because this is precisely where we are now seeing the disclosure of what is called the Holy Spirit's plan, the action of the Spirit in history.

Providence and ideologies

So what is history? Up till recently, people were content to live in their own times. They were faced with tasks to be done, greater or smaller, according to their place in society, their culture, their office, from the humble artisan to the king or the head of state. From the lowest to the highest, they were all men with their burden of misery, ignorance and ambition. There were geniuses who did good and there were also tyrants and mediocre thinkers. But modern man is no longer content with this attitude.

[21]'He who abides in me, and I in him, he it is that bears much fruit, for apart from me you can do nothing.' Jn. 15:5

He feels that from now on man cannot take charge of his own history and construct his own future, unless he is able to grasp the laws of history, either to overcome them or direct them better, or even serve them better, according to his conception of 'history' and human evolution. These thought systems gave rise to what are called ideologies. Here we are faced with an enterprise which is both important and dangerous, because man cannot really grasp history in a scientific way. He runs the risk of error and in fact he makes mistakes, or he reduces his own history to the unfolding of a certain type of relationships, sometimes nearly exclusively economic.

This has led Christians to reflect. All round them they find this reading of history to discover its laws, the better to direct them and to be in control of the building of the future. The Christian wants to see God's hand in this building. Is not history directed by what used to be called God's Providence? Is not Christ the Lord and Master of history? Of course he is. But is not it equally dangerous for the Christian to claim that he is capable of grasping *God's* plan? How can he know what this is? Or if he does discover it, will he forget his own responsibilities and lose sight of the fact that history is full of greatness and misery, horror, cruelty, oppression, as well as good actions, and will continue to be so in the future?

Are we capable of discerning God's will and discovering the part played by the work of the Spirit of God in the shaping of events? This is called 'reading' events. There is a temptation for Christians to believe that they have a grasp of history as Christians. I do not intend to discuss this enormous subject at length but merely to state the problem, which is very important.

The christian attempt to see God working in history is based on a sound intuition but at the same time there is a grave risk of making mistakes and seeing God's plan in an anthropomorphic manner, leading us to imagine God's action in accordance with our own limited and rational concepts. No doubt God knows where we are going. However, Jesus himself, as man, seems to say that he does not know. This was an astonishing answer he gave the apostles when they asked him about the end of the world. Jesus as a prophet, using prophetical language, described a vision without perspective, like all prophetic visions. It referred at the same time to the destruction of Jerusalem, the future of the kingdom of Israel and the end of the world. When the apostles asked him when these things would be, Jesus answered that even the Son of man did not know, but only the Father.[22] I think we should take literally these words of Jesus who was still in his earthly state. The timing of these events was probably not expressible in human words and concepts.

It is absolutely beyond man's power to formulate a precise conception of the evolution of history, so that we can take charge of the unfolding of a divine plan which we claim to have discerned. How could this be possible? First we would have to be clear about what we mean by an event. The term has a precise meaning in a certain philosophy of history. The question is whether this interpretation of the 'event' is the true one. The fact that this interpretation gives rise to a philosophy of history whence an immediately effective political practice is derived is not a criterion for its truth. Or else we are no longer speaking the same truth.

As against the christian faith in the mystery of the Kingdom of God, there is a materialist vision of history, the vision of those who do not believe that beyond history, beyond mankind, beyond the lives of human beings, there exists a Being who is completely free, personal and capable of love. This sovereign freedom of God who is Love and therefore personal, justifies the price man must pay to remain free and to struggle constantly to free himself. This God is also the justification for the supreme value of love, so that man cannot be content with a mediocre love, and

[22]'But of that day and hour no one knows, not even the angels of heaven, nor the Son, but the Father only.' Matt. 24:36

the search for this love is the driving force of his actions even in the social order. No, I do not think we can know anything about mankind's final end, apart from what Jesus told us and from heeding the commandment of the Gospel to seek justice and love continually.

Those who claim to be able to see the future of mankind, by means of science, go beyond the scope of science. Meteorologists are able to predict the weather one or two days beforehand, and competent scientists think that with the increased observation points provided by spatial laboratories it might be possible to predict the weather a week in advance. But beyond that, they say it is not possible, human science cannot see further than this because of the extreme variability and complexity of the factors involved.

The respect that Christians should have for God's secret plan for history and their refusal to identify this plan with any ideological project, does not keep Jesus' disciples apart from the real construction of history to come. It should make them determined never to set limits on the effort necessary for the improvement of human societies. They should be realistic and competent and can of course unite their efforts with those of other men of good will, to establish the kind of society that seems best in given historical circumstances. But they know that the Gospel calls on them constantly to go beyond the limits and degradations of human systems, constantly to demand a development of institutions to make them better fitted to promoting peace, justice and brotherhood between men. Christ's disciples, even when they join in a plan for society and collaborate with others, must always be prepared for constant readjustments and changes, even radical ones. Christians always remain free and not bound by any society whatever, because they cannot stop always demanding more love and justice. Thus through the Gospel they are the leaven of love and peace in the human dough, the salt of justice and liberation from all oppression. How can this not be obvious to every disciple of the Lord Jesus?

Mao and Theresa of the Child Jesus

So what must we say about the history of mankind? For men are not conditioned to the extent that they are no longer capable, by their free decisions, of changing the course of history in an unforeseeable manner.[23] Or are we slaves forever to blind destiny? No, because there exists another universe besides the universe of events: every human being has a heart, a spirit and a conscience. This is true of every human being, whatever he does. Whatever their activities, a mother looking after her children, a nun at prayer, a politician at work, or a member of a communist party committee, all these people have a heart, a spirit and a conscience. And this is where God is present and active in a mysterious way, and this is the reign of the Spirit. God is present through his Spirit but we are rarely conscious of it. Yes, God's Spirit is present. And those who believe in Jesus know that the Spirit of Christ is in them since their baptism and that they have this special gift of baptism of being guided by the Spirit of adoption. It is therefore true to say that in human action, whether in private and personal life or in collective or political projects, man is a divine creature but he must still rely on his own judgment. We are all left to our own devices, even when we are moved by the Spirit of Christ.

It is interesting to compare the work and influence of a man like Mao and of a girl like Theresa of the Child Jesus. Compare these two characters: both achieved a work of love, a work of intelligence. How can we discern what was done under the impulse of the Holy Spirit? I make this comparison because it was said at a christian assembly that Mao's revolution was a manifestation of the Holy Spirit. Jesus told us that we would know the tree by its fruits. 'Every sound tree bears good fruit, but the bad tree

[23]A typical example is the unforeseeable development of the enormous country of China: Mao by his decisions and actions was the agent of an economic and political change that no one could have foreseen. China did not have the conditions foreseen by marxist-leninism as necessary to the success of a revolution.

bears evil fruit. A sound tree cannot bear evil fruit, nor can a bad tree bear good fruit.'[24] This is a clear and simple statement and in the discernment of the action of the Holy Spirit, it is now more useful than ever. Is there a difference between the reign of the Holy Spirit in the heart of a baptized person who has faith in Christ, and the reign of the Holy Spirit in the heart of a materialist who rejects the christian faith? There is a level of depth in the life of the human spirit which we cannot plumb. I do not know the answer to this question. I know that no one is abandoned by God, but also that a man can close the doors of his mind to the divine light, through pride of reason or a refusal of transcendence, and that a man can also close the doors of his heart through hatred, love of money or ambition.

However, I believe that the Spirit sent by Jesus, whom he himself called the Paraclete, the Spirit of light who comforts and enlightens the disciples in their faith, in what has been revealed to them about the mystery of God in Christ, this Spirit communicates a knowledge of God and a freedom of love which is proper to the reign of the Spirit in the Church, the reign of the Kingdom of God. This action of the Spirit is different from the way in which the Spirit of God accompanies every man, even the unbeliever. Did not Jesus say that the world was not capable of receiving the Spirit of Truth promised to the apostles 'because it does not see him and does not know him'?[25] The Spirit of adoption can only be manifested in him who knows that by baptism he is dead with Christ and reborn with Christ to a new life. The disciples of Jesus baptize in the Holy Spirit.[26]

And when I compared Mao to Theresa it was to compare the repercussion each of these two types of life had on the rest of mankind. I do not think Mao would have been

[24]Matt. 7:17–18
[25]Jn. 14:16–17
[26]Matt. 3:11; 28:19

interested in Theresa of the Child Jesus! Their sphere of action and view of humanity was completely different. I mean it: completely different. This is what makes us realize that there is a choice to be made. You have chosen the way of Theresa of Lisieux. Are you aware that you have this choice? Because there is a choice to be made. Mao is a good representative of a certain conception of the perfection of man, a man who seemed to open a new way to lead a society out of the impossible and inhuman dead-end that others had led it into, by error, ignorance or by their inability to control a situation which had become too complicated.

Now we must speak of the action of the Spirit of adoption in the heart of every Christian. The extraordinary thing that sometimes shocks us is that people find it easy to accept a collective idea of human good, even if this good must be paid for at the cost of the freedom of conscience of millions of human beings. In this light we no longer know whether it is man who must serve a sort of ideological 'Being', often at the cost of real slavery to this 'Absolute', or whether the coming of this ideological society is really necessary for men to become free. We do not know. But when we speak of the Spirit of adoption sent by Jesus, we are speaking of a close and intimate relationship between every man, who has become a child of God, with the Trinity, with the Father. The divine life cannot be collective. Perhaps that is why it does not interest those who only care about collective things and political realities. I will not repeat what I said about the repercussions that Christ's resurrection and his transfigured humanity working through the Church and its members can and ought to have on the history of the world, even in the political sphere.

Now we have spoken about this reign of the Holy Spirit, we must talk about how it is manifested in the community of the Church, in prayer, in the relationship between the individual and God. The renewal of the Spirit we hear about nowadays works on this level. Whether we mean

70

charismatic movements or the thirst for prayer and contemplation that drives so many men and women to renounce a materialist society—without knowing how to change this society—and go to live in the desert, this renewal manifests a special action of the Holy Spirit and requires true discernment. Is it right that some people should give up trying to accomplish urgent human tasks? So we must ask ourselves about the life of prayer, the knowledge of God in the Holy Spirit, and about the religious vocation, which is also on this level.

VI

The Kingdom of God Does Not Come Like a Visible Fact

Now we are going to speak about the reign of the Holy Spirit in human hearts. This is not easy, it is difficult to see clearly here because of the very humility of God's action, its invisibility. Furthermore, God's support to our freedom, the power that is given us, the light of truth that enlightens us, all that we call the action of the Holy Spirit in us, is usually not discernible. We know that in committing ourselves to the way of the Gospel and to a christian or religious life, we are committing ourselves to a work we cannot accomplish without the help of the Spirit of Jesus. Religious when they take their final vows are aware that such an act cannot be undertaken except in the trust and hope that the Holy Spirit will not fail them, so that they should not be afraid of their own weakness. But in daily life we constantly experience this weakness. This is true both of religious and other Christians. No doubt we feel almost certain sometimes that the Lord is with us, that he has given us a great light. There are indeed moments in our lives when we cannot doubt that God has intervened, even though we may not be able to explain why: we see our lives in a new light, we feel sure in our hearts that the Lord has called us, either to be converted to a christian life or to dedicate ourselves to him in a religious order. But unfortunately, things are not always as clear as this. Then we feel that we are left all on our own.

This is true not only for each of us as individuals, but

also for religious orders. There is enthusiasm for a new foundation under difficult conditions, and by the power of obedience people feel they can dare anything. And then sometimes the feeling changes. Everything breaks down. Members' health breaks down, there are difficulties within the community. Then there is the temptation to fall from a state of spiritual euphoria into depression, and this is what often happens because this is the way we usually behave in life. We can tell ourselves again and again that we could have foreseen that trials would come—this does not stop our mood from changing.

The same happens when we are praying. There are days of inner expansion when our spirit feels bathed in light and certainty, where everything seems lovely and easy and we feel kindly towards everyone. When we feel this it is hard for us to believe others who remind us that perhaps this mood will not last and that we should prepare ourselves for darkness and difficulties.

This is also true of the founding of an order. There is the period at the beginning when the foundation seems like an admirable work of the Holy Spirit. This is true of most of the charismatic movements in the Church. When we examine the history of these movements, the ones that were really caused by the Holy Spirit, we find that they are subject to the ordinary laws of all human institutions: enthusiasm at the beginning, a falling away, the need for reform, renewal, ageing and sometimes disappearance. This is true of every institution in the Church. Some people would like to see clearer signs of God's help and action. There will always be reason for criticizing the Church, because we will always be able to find imperfections in it, things that are no longer adapted to its aims. We could also criticize every christian or religious community, and of course each of our own lives. We are no better than others.

But we can also look at the Church in a different way. The Church gave birth to the saints who are the manifestations of Christ's active presence in his Body which is this

Church with a human face. And above all there is God's invisible action, which cannot be seen from outside. Among the crowds that go to Lourdes there are no doubt people who are seeking miracles and spectacular cures. When these happen—which is rare—they are not very spectacular. Miracles require years and years of medical scrutiny before they are accepted as such by the Church. But the priests who hear confessions at Lourdes know what goes on in people's hearts—the conversions, the wonderful changes, the really new lives. This is the true divine action of the Spirit. But this action is not visible and it takes place deep down inside where God alone can intervene.

Nowadays we hear a lot about a charismatic renewal which is a sort of visible bubbling of the Holy Spirit. First we should reflect on the nature of the phenomena which are thus described. For in order to have the right idea about the relationship between God and man, we must be aware of what God wants to make of us and of what we are, earthly human creatures. It is not easy to speak of these things because we keep having to say the opposite of what we have just said! On the one hand, we must insist on the personal responsibility of the believer, his initiative; and on the other, we must insist on the power and initiative of the action of the Spirit which is often invisible.

If we want to think about the reign of the Holy Spirit after Christ's coming, we should start with the personal life of each of Christ's disciples. Each Christian is invited to read the Gospel and to change his life by putting it into practice, so that he lives here below as a son of God, particularly in the relationship of love and friendship he should have with his Father in heaven.

We can also think of the action of the Holy Spirit in the building of christian communities where God constantly gathers together believers in the unity of faith and deep brotherly communion. First there is each christian community and then the larger more universal community of the Church, Christ's presence, often almost invisible but still real, among mankind.

74

Lastly there is the divine government of the world in its historical development. There has been a sort of language slide on this subject. People used to talk about the rule of Providence, but nowadays the term is hardly ever used. We prefer to talk about the plans of the Spirit. As we have seen, we ought to think in terms of trying to discern the Spirit of God's plans in history. Fundamentally we are still talking about the same reality, although our contemporaries think they have discovered something new. This language change can cause confusion, because the Spirit's reign in history and the Spirit's reign in believers' hearts is spoken of without distinguishing the term. The idea of Providence distinguished a different reality in the history of creation from that of the Kingdom of God. I simply make this remark in passing.

Internalizing the divine law

Let us now speak about our intimate personal lives in their relationship with the Spirit. What goes on in us? We are Jesus' disciples and we know he asks us radically to change our lives. We have only to read the Gospel to know this. Jesus expects something of man, he offers us an ideal which I cannot describe without referring to the Gospel as a whole. Today I do not want to speak about this ideal Jesus offers us but about the part the Holy Spirit promised by Jesus has to play in this work of transformation.

In the history of christian spirituality there have always been two interwoven tendencies: either the stress is laid on God's action and a certain passivity of man under the influence of this action with the emphasis on man's inadequacy, or the stress is on man's responsibility, the freedom and power of his will. We cannot easily reconcile the two, because we cannot see how our freedom can be strengthened, enlightened, guided by the Spirit of God without ceasing to be *our* freedom. We also find it difficult to balance this freedom with keeping the law, the law of Jesus, which we are bound to obey.

The Sermon on the Mount as reported by Matthew gives us a summary of Christ's commandments defining the ideal he offers his disciples. This is the gospel man we should try to become. We should constantly compare what we are with the ideal Jesus sets before us. We must strive to become this gospel man. This is something we must do as well as we can. Jesus said clearly: 'You are my friends if you do what I command you.'[1] And once he even complained about the apostles' disobedience: 'Why do you call me "Lord, Lord", and not do what I tell you?'[2]

It is not enough for us to believe in Christ, or to listen to his teaching, or to wait confidently for him to reform us, we must do what he tells us. Of course, this depends on our free will. And when Jesus asks someone to follow him, he adds 'if you want to'. When he cures the sick or receives a profession of faith from certain sinners who say they want to change, he says: 'Go and sin no more.' Jesus leaves it up to them. However, there are sayings by Christ which seem to contradict this, when he says for example: 'Without me you can do nothing' or 'With men this is impossible, but with God all things are possible.'[3] What does this mean? Jesus never says that we must not strive, we must not make our own efforts. He says: 'Without me you can do nothing.' The question is what things cannot we do without him. We will keep coming back to this question.

Jesus is saying the same thing in other words when he compares himself to a vine and the sap which circulates through the trunk and the branches which are the disciples.[4] If we, the branches, are cut off from the main stem, we wither and die. It is quite clear that Jesus is not speaking here about our ability to act effectively in human matters. People can do all sorts of things without Christ's help.

[1]Jn. 15:14
[2]Lk. 6:46
[3]Matt. 19:26; Lk. 18:27
[4]Jn. 15:1–6

They are free, they have free will, powers, they can act with intelligence, conceive plans, fulfil them and even change themselves. Christ is speaking about a degree or quality of change which permeates everything, which is like a leaven in our lives and makes us like Christ and behave like children of God. We can only do this in and with the Spirit.[5]

The first thing we must do if we have decided to follow Jesus is prepare ourselves to do what he tells us. This requires an internalization of the divine law. God can see into the depths of our hearts and Jesus asks us to obey him even in our thoughts and most secret desires. He repeated some of the commandments of the law given by God to Moses on Sinai and at the same time deepened their scope. Thus on adultery: 'You have heard that it was said, "You shall not commit adultery." But I say to you that everyone who looks at a woman lustfully has already committed adultery with her in his heart.'[6] This is what I mean by the internalization of the law. Christ's law covers not only external acts but also internal acts, which other people cannot see and apparently have no external consequences.

Then there is freedom from the law. I speak of this here because it all hangs together. This idea of the freedom of the children of God is sometimes abused; it is thought of as freedom from the law without being very clear what this means. We are given the impression that each of us may decide on his own way in total freedom, and that the law is merely a directive to be interpreted according to the situation. This attitude corresponds to the general mentality of a society called permissive, where each person must decide what is good or better on his own personal responsibility. Each person must act in accordance with his own conscience, his conscience is respected and in fact regarded as autonomous. This makes the human individual con-

[5]'God has sent the Spirit of his Son into our hearts, crying, "Abba! Father!" ' Gal. 4:6; cf. also Rom. 8:15
[6]Matt. 5:27

science the supreme criterion, even if its decision is not in accordance with the Gospel. Of course conscience is conscience and none of us can judge another's. However, each of us is responsible for his own conscience and it is a mistake to deny this responsibility.

In fact, the object of the divine law and the teachings of Jesus is precisely to educate the disciples' consciences. The psalms speak admirably of the conscience of the just man among the Jewish people before the coming of Christ. The law given by God to his people and through them to all mankind, the Ten Commandments particularized in a body of customs and prescriptions, was intended to change the heart of every man in Israel. It was not supposed to be imposed from without but written on the heart. The law should be assimilated to the point when it became free consent. Psalm 118, the longest in the psalter, is typical in this respect. It can be wearisome at first reading, because each verse just repeats the same ideas in different ways and with different words. Pascal said this was his favourite psalm. The more you get to know this psalm—it is broken up in the new Office—the more you will meditate on its main theme which is the assimilation of the divine law; the law is my life, so I should assimilate it. What does this mean? Personal assimilation of the law means making it your own, and this is what turns the law into freedom when it would otherwise be an external constraint upon freedom.

Let us take an example: the highway code. In some places you must not go faster than 30 mph. You can keep this rule because you do not want to be fined or lose your licence and thus you will exceed the speed limit whenever you are sure you can do so without being caught. You decide when and whether to obey this law, whenever you are sure you will not get caught. There is another possible attitude which is deciding that the speed limit is reasonable and that it does help decrease the number of road accidents. In this case, you are no longer worried about the penalties of breaking it, it is no longer a constraint because you have assimilated and made a personal decision to keep it.

The same is true of the divine law. We should not keep the divine law because we fear punishment, or just because it is a law, but since Christ has shown us that the object of the commandments is love, love of God and our fellows has become the reason why we obey the law. Love must teach me to obey God's precepts. I must assimilate God's law to the point where I can no longer think otherwise. Then I am free! Do you imagine Jesus took liberties with the divine law? This is quite unthinkable. He was the Father's Son, he freely and truly loved men his brothers and God his Father. That is why he is master of the law and its ordinances, as he said about the sabbath: 'For the Son of man is lord of the sabbath.'[7] He did not disobey the divine law of the sabbath but he put this law of sacred rest which had been given for man's good and service in its proper place. Jesus took as an example the apostles' action when they were hungry and picked ears of corn in a field, rubbed them and ate them on the sabbath day. It was prohibitions like these which weighed down the law, and disfigured its meaning that Jesus denounced as a betrayal of the lawgiver's intentions. But Jesus did not abolish the law of the sabbath.

Like Jesus, the Christian must free himself by making the divine law his own, in its purest and deepest sense, because he has understood the law's divine intention, revealed by Jesus, love.

This attitude needs a clear-sighted conscience and freedom in ourselves which can only come from the habit of renunciation, because each of us has passions and instinctive habits which lead us to interpret the law differently. This is a false notion of true freedom. Because of our limitations and ignorance, and because we are not always in this state of inner freedom, we often have to accept the duty of keeping the law just because it is a law and God's

[7]Matt. 12:8

law, even if in a particular case we cannot see the reason for it.

I do not need to remind you that there are some situations in which it is very painful for us to keep the law, which may then seem too hard or even inhuman to us. Yes, working to make the law's logic our own means gaining christian freedom, the true freedom of love, but not any sort of love. It is easy to mock at the law's demands and to side with human weakness. St Augustine's phrase 'Love and do as you will' is often misused by taking it out of context and distorting its meaning. The whole point is what 'love' and what 'will' Augustine means.

Cardinal Journet and Jacques Duclos

Keeping Christ's law also raises other questions, because there is the feeling of love and acts of love. There is the level of actions and works, and the level of heart and feeling. In fact there are actions, attitudes and even institutions normally expressive of love we have for our fellow men and which can even be ordained by law in a particular society for the common good. Individual men and women can dedicate their lives to doing works of justice and love, with generosity and competence. Some may even do great service to mankind but that does not necessarily mean that their hearts have been transformed by love. Nowadays people are cautious of holiness of heart, calling it 'personalism' in a pejorative sense, just as they call the inner requirements of christian holiness, the heart's secrets which God alone sees, 'intimism'. Of course we could rightly criticize as intimist a self-centred attitude which enclosed us within ourselves. But if we behaved like this we would no longer do acts and works of love. The apostle James strongly attacked this illusion.[8] But there is another idea of

[8]'What does it profit, my brethren, if a man says he has faith but has not works?' Jas. 2:14

perfection which only values effective service of our neigh-
bour, without bothering about what is happening in our
hearts. This kind of perfection by its nature can even be
imposed by the State on the citizens of a collectivist society.

I think I gave you an example of these types of perfection
in one of my letters, when I spoke about the death of two
very different men: Cardinal Journet and Jacques Duclos.
I was struck by the difference because they died very close
together.

The Abbé Journet was a man of God whose holiness
could only be felt by those near him. He died in great
poverty. At his funeral people from every walk of life, poor
people as well as theologians, gathered to pay their respects
to this man of God. His holiness was all within him, it was
humility, faith and prayer.

Jacques Duclos was a very good man during his lifetime.
He was generous and disinterested and all his efforts were
dedicated to the Trade Union struggle and to the good of
the working class. There was a huge crowd at his funeral.
This man was an atheist.

These are two different examples of human perfection.
One had considerable effect on workers' lives through his
activities and political struggles, while the other remained
hidden in God's mystery and bore the fruits of wisdom in
theological works in the services of the Church.

These are two extreme examples which I have quoted
because they illustrate the problem facing many Christians
today. Of course there is no opposition in principle between
these two types of perfection. But frequently there is opposition in fact, because someone who is much concerned
with his personal life and perfection can become timid in
outside activities, even those connected with his vocation.
Whereas those who are very busy doing good works often
find they must sacrifice other moral values, for example
family life and relationships with friends. Few people, even
Christians, really attach importance to purity of heart and
imagination.

Yes, there are two types of perfection. We cannot avoid

the question of how deep the change in our lives should go through Christ's life in us. There are works and there are intentions. There are socially effective works and the heart's attitudes and feelings.

The difficulties we run into in our attempts to love are of all kinds. That is why we try to change because we have become aware of the Lord's love which urges us and we cannot rest in peace until we have done all we can. And when it comes to loving other people we come up against the complex problem of social relationships. We all know how difficult these can be.

We find ourselves in the situation described so well by the apostle Paul when he contrasted the old man with the new man. We must all undergo the paschal mystery, that is to say the passover from death to life. We cannot avoid having to die to ourselves, 'denying' ourselves, to use Christ's expression. But what does 'dying to ourselves' mean?

Jesus spoke about it in words difficult to interpret: 'Whoever seeks to gain his life will lose it, but whoever loses his life will preserve it.'[9] We must therefore accept this double mystery in us of death and new life. This is what St Paul is saying when he says, that he no longer lives but Christ lives in him.[10] The Spirit of Christ is at work in the apostle. He was an active, enterprising man, a bold witness to the Gospel, but at the same time he was a contemplator of Christ living in him. For Paul this inner transformation was the chief work of the Spirit sent by Christ glorified. This same life of the Holy Spirit takes place in each one of us.

'My grace is sufficient for you'

But how can this work of the Spirit be real, when we feel we are left to rely on our own strength? Paul felt the same

[9]Lk. 17:33. This message is repeated six times in the Gospels: Jn. 12:25; Matt. 10:39; 16:25; Mk. 8:35; Lk. 9:24
[10]'It is no longer I who live, but Christ who lives in me.' Gal. 2:20

82

and sometimes he complained to the Lord about it when he felt he could not go on: 'And to keep me from being too elated by the abundance of revelations, a thorn was given me in the flesh, a messenger of Satan, to harass me, to keep me from being too elated.'[11] We do not know what Paul is referring to, but it must be some very humiliating weakness in his human nature. 'Three times I besought the Lord about this, that it should leave me; but he said to me, "My grace is sufficient for you." ' But in one sense God's grace is not sufficient because Paul is not delivered from his weakness! But it is in this struggle that the work of Christ is done, and this is what we find so difficult to accept. . . ! Then prayer arises because of this conflict which makes us feel that we are left to our own strength on the one hand, and that on the other Christ asks us to count on his power, a power whose force we seldom feel!

Some days we might feel like telling ourselves: 'It's not surprising that I can't manage, because Jesus says that without him we can do nothing!' Or we blame ourselves that we are not subject enough to Christ's influence, because we feel no change in ourselves. Yes, we should complain to Christ, pray like the apostle Paul. This is not an easy attitude to take, because it requires us both not to accept the evil in us and to feel humble in our weakness. It is a reality of ourselves we cannot fathom, whereas at the conscious level, we are in permanent contradiction. St Paul also says: 'I can do all things in him who strengthens me.'[12] But the weakness remains. He can do all things but he does not succeed in mastering himself completely. He is obliged to admit that he does what he does not want to do and does not manage to do what he wants to do.[13] He even speaks of this 'body of death' and asks to be delivered from it.[14]

[11]II Cor. 12:7–10
[12]Phil. 4:13
[13]'I do not understand my own actions. For I do not do what I want, but I do the very thing I hate.' Rom. 7:15
[14]Rom. 7:24

All these contradictions should not shock or discourage us. They belong to the human condition. We bear within us a conflict that will go on all our lives.

We must be attentive to the Lord's presence because we do not know what we would become without him. This brings us to a further realization: we cannot discern the Spirit's presence in us, except perhaps on a few rare occasions and especially when we receive insights from him about his divine Being or the hidden meaning of his Word. As we have said, the gifts of the Spirit have been given to us and are at work in us, usually without our being aware of it.

Brother Charles was very conscious of the need to be helped by the Spirit of love, who is the Holy Spirit. That is why he recited the 'Veni Creator' every day. He sometimes even sang it alone. I think this was the only prayer he sang. He admitted that he could not sing in tune, but as there was no one to hear him, he wanted to sing to express the power of this invocation to the Holy Spirit, he wanted it to be solemn and universal. He invoked the Spirit for his personal transformation, faithfulness to Christ, the fulfilling of the Gospel in his life, but also that all people might be saved.

Of course an unbeliever could well be sceptical of such a recourse to the Spirit, because, seen from the outside, the action attributed to the Spirit has few visible results. In the history of the Church, the manifestations of this reign of the Spirit are neither spectacular nor even visible to unbelieving eyes. The Church is itself subject to the human condition and its limitations. We cannot escape from the laws of our humanity with all its weaknesses, possibilities of error and sin. We must never forget this.

When we speak of christian life, the transformation it should work within us in the light of Christ and the power of his Spirit of love, we have plenty of reasons to give way to the need for a certain realism—because this is reality!—and doubt the effectiveness of the Spirit of God. This attitude makes us timid and unself-confident, we may grow discouraged and feel there is nothing to be done, we shall never change! Or we may be deluded by a kind of idealism, imagining that the action of the Spirit will enable us to fulfil the christian ideal, in spite of ourselves. Then we are disappointed nearly every day, we force ourselves to keep up our courage in the hope of some radical change, and in the end we do not know what to think! On the one hand we tell ourselves that we must keep going, we must not give up. On the other we tell ourselves that the Lord knows our weakness and accepts us as we are. . . ! The apostle Paul realizes this and Christ answers him: 'My power is made perfect in weakness.'[15] But we would like things to be a bit clearer, the action of the Spirit to be a bit more obvious, and the Spirit to tell us what he expects of us, what he is doing in us that we cannot see. But he does not tell us. In all lives there are periods of light and periods of darkness, even when the Holy Spirit enlightens us, except in certain exceptional circumstances. This light comes to us because we have wanted it and sought for it.

You would be wrong to take the Gospel to meditate on saying there is no point in learning more by reflection and study in order to understand Christ's words better; you would be wrong not to take the trouble to meditate on the Gospel with the help of a sound exegesis because you expected the Holy Spirit to enlighten you without it. The same is true of your conscience. Some days you will feel that the Holy Spirit suggested a certain idea of decision to you. But you ask why should it necessarily come from the Holy Spirit? I could quite easily answer you that it was you who had had the idea by your own thinking. We must be careful when we speak about this, because whatever the Lord does in us, he will never relieve us of our personal responsibility as free human beings.

We have a duty to act on our own judgment, we must think what we should do to act for the best in everything.

[15]'My grace is sufficient for you, for my power is made perfect in weakness.' II Cor. 12:9

Look how Paul behaved in the founding of churches. He ran into numerous difficulties which he struggled to resolve by right judgment and thoughtful decisions. We are never dispensed from the need to think for ourselves because we are waiting for the help of the Holy Spirit. We are never dispensed from respecting human means or from using them in the proper way. Anything involving a decrease in human value and responsibility would be a false interpretation of the reign of the Holy Spirit.

However, our resistance to the Holy Spirit is not usually out of respect for the proper role of our mind and will. The obstacles are much more likely to be pride, the desire for power, an immoderate self-confidence. This attitude closes our eyes to the light of the Spirit and delivers us over to all our human weaknesses, just when we think we are powerful. We should not forget that the Holy Spirit is God, a God we should respect. We should not ascribe to his intervention any idea that comes into our heads! If you tell me that the Holy Spirit has suggested such and such an idea to you, I reply: 'What is it? Tell me your idea and let us see whether it is good and reasonable or not.' 'The tree is judged by its fruits,' said the Lord.[16] And how can we judge whether a fruit is good? By our common sense and sound judgment, of course! But clear judgment requires inner freedom. Anyone who is enslaved by his desires or passions is not free within and his judgment cannot be sound.[17]

Called to love

Prayer arises from the depths of ourselves, it is a cry of our weakness seeking the power of the Spirit, a cry in darkness seeking light. In the sight of God we are really powerless and ignorant in one sphere, that of the revelation of the secret of God's inner life, the manifestation of the Son in

[16]Matt. 7:20
[17]'For every one who does evil hates the light . . .' Jn. 3:20; 'If your eye is not sound, your whole body will be full of darkness.' Matt. 6:23

Jesus Christ, and through him the manifestation of the Father. This secret is accessible only to the Holy Spirit. Who can tell us about God except him who comes from God?[18] And here Christ's words which we quoted are literally true: 'Without me you can do nothing.'[19] Yes, in all matters concerning the Kingdom of God which Jesus came to reveal to us, we can do nothing without him, because he alone knows its secrets. And in order to prepare ourselves for this Kingdom, in order to be able to receive it, we must go on a long inner pilgrimage of humility, self-conquest, so that we are open to the light that comes from beyond reason, to love, to childlike faith.

Thus it is important to distinguish these spheres, even if they overlap. The distinction between them does not affect the unity of our being or our life, but it reminds us that in this life there are different levels and that the final unity of our being can only be attained in the transcendence of the Kingdom of God.

Above all, there is the revelation of the mystery of God as Father, a revelation we can only fully receive from the Spirit of God. The apostle Paul tells us that we can only address God as 'Abba, Father', by virtue of the Spirit of adoption which has been given to us. He alone enables us to relate to God as his children. He alone has shown us in Christ the mystery of the Father's love and mercy.

Then together with this revelation of God's mystery, there is the mission that God has given his Church and to Christians to make known their mystery in their turn. In this too the Spirit asks for our initiative, our intelligence, although we cannot separate ourselves from the Spirit who sent us if we are to accomplish this mission.

Finally the third work of the reign of the Spirit is the gathering of the community of Christians into the Church. Every christian community, be it local church or religious order, has been gathered together by the Holy Spirit in

[18]Jn. 1:18; 8:38
[19]Jn. 15:5

Christ's name and the reality of his glorified humanity, even when this community constantly runs into difficulties and problems common to every human group, even if the motives and aims of this community are different.

To conclude this chapter I return to the consequences of these two almost contradictory aspects, of effectiveness and ineffectiveness, that characterize the progress and transformation of human beings: human beings in fact depend on various things, such as upbringing and everything that contributes through love to the transformation of the heart and emotions. These two contributory factors, the action of the Spirit and human endeavour, strengthen one another. Ideologies now in power struggle, sometimes by violence, to acquire a monopoly of the means of bringing up children, because they are convinced that man can only be changed if he is influenced by his upbringing from his earliest years. Because of this, some regimes achieve spectactular results, not only with children but also with the adult masses.

I am alluding here to the collective disciplines, scientifically studied to transform human behaviour at the level of social relationships. And this is indeed a quicker way to create a new type of human being, who is open to others, cares about the common good and is devoted to the work of building the city. These political pressure techniques can affect whole populations, whereas Christ's messengers of the Gospel preach in the wilderness and apparently get very few results. For calling people to love, in freedom, does not get quick results.

VII

The Spirit's Secret Work in the Heart of Man

When we spoke of the work of the Spirit in us, I pointed out that it was impossible to define his action in general because it is infinitely personal and unique in each human life. The Spirit has as many modes of action as there are people in the world. We are aware of our own unique self, our life is like no one else's and our inner life is also unique. The action in us of the Holy Spirit is also unique; he is closer to us than we are to ourselves, because we live on a conscious level but the Spirit of God the Creator penetrates the most secret layers of our being. No one can foresee or describe the Spirit's action in the depth of his being. Of course we can note certain aspects or characteristics of this divine work in man. But it is more important for us to know how we can help this action, or more precisely, collaborate with it. God's action never destroys our freedom. On the contrary, it strengthens it by his Spirit.

In the Gospel we find a terrible saying of Christ's. He came to reveal his Father's mercy, he forgave his torturers, he told all the poor who came to bewail their sins at his feet that God forgave them, he said he had not come to condemn the world but to save it.[1] In one thing only Jesus seems hard, that is when he is speaking of the sin against the Spirit which will never be forgiven.[2] This sin cannot be

[1] Jn. 3:17
[2] Mk. 3:29

forgiven because it is a rebellion against the Spirit of God. Forgiveness can only reach a heart prepared to accept it. This sin is a refusal to be forgiven. Thus Jesus shows us how the Spirit is with us, penetrating the heart of our will without ever destroying our freedom; otherwise we would be neither human nor children capable of loving God our Father. The Spirit's personal action on each of us is invisible to us and to others. However, when we think back over our lives, there are days when we have the impression that we were really guided by Providence. Certain events were decisive or providential for us. In themselves they may not have been important but their effect on us was profound. Other events may have given us a severe shock, like the death of a loved one, and this shock, by the grace of the Spirit, had a profound effect on us, turning our lives upside down, whereas a similar event on another occasion might not have had such an effect. So it was not the event in itself but our reaction to it which was the decisive factor in the change it brought about in us. It can also be an illness which changes us in this way, whereas the same trial might not have the same effect on others or on us in other circumstances. What converts one person disgusts another. There are lives which have been radically changed by a meeting or a few words. The experience of poverty can give rise to a vocation of dedication to the service of the poorest. We call these events providential. In fact these events are usually the result of a chain of circumstances we call chance. The same events might have very different, even opposite effects on different people. It is easy to find examples in each of our lives.

I quote as an example the birth of the Abbé Pierre's vocation to work for tramps. The beginning was a meteorological event—a very hard winter. It was especially hard for the tramps who usually slept under bridges or at tube station entrances. I do not remember the circumstances in which the Abbé Pierre, who was an M.P., was induced to broadcast an appeal on the radio which set everything going. This was the beginning of a complete change in his life, which from then on was dedicated to the tramps, whereas others might have been content to work for them only as long as the cold weather lasted. We could always find natural causes for every event, but deep in our hearts there are the decisions taken by our freedom in the freedom of the Holy Spirit, whose action remains invisible and its consequences unpredictable.

Unbelievers are quite free to interpret events without ever discerning any trace of the intervention of the Holy Spirit, because his action never works directly on events, but in the secret of human hearts reacting freely to these events. Nowadays we often hear the expression that events 'challenge' us. This is true, we should feel challenged by events, but it would be more accurate to say that in the face of events we should challenge ourselves. We should not think of every event as having meaning in itself. An earthquake, for example, is a consequence of the laws of geological evolution of the earth. But when it destroys a whole town and causes a human disaster, we must consider how to react to it. Christians must consider what behaviour is most in accordance with the Gospel and God's will in the face of historical situations. Some will go further than others, because here we are in the mysterious region of consciences, where a light or an impulse from the Spirit of God can change a whole life. Some people are driven to blaspheme against Providence and rebel against God because of the misfortunes in their lives, because of the existence of evil in the world, whereas others, like some of the saints, sing of God's wonders and praise Providence, even when they are suffering misfortune. Are their eyes closed to people's sufferings? Are they concerned with nothing but the joy the Lord has given them in their hearts?

We must strive to be like Christ, the perfect man. Christ looked at the world clearly, saw all the evil of human suffering and died of it. The evangelist tells us that Jesus did not need to be told about anyone because he knew what was in men's hearts,[3] which explains some of his behaviour to people that society looked at askance. He knew. Christ saw clearly and realistically but this did not prevent him from proclaiming: 'Blessed are the poor, blessed are those who mourn, blessed are the hungry, blessed are those who are persecuted.'[4] These are called the beatitudes. Perhaps they should have been called the misfortunes.

We too often think of the beatitudes as a way to be followed, a life programme. But Christ did not say this. He was simply stating what he saw. The poor are not happy, those who suffer persecution are not happy, but what we must discover, as the saints did, often from their own experience, is that through misfortune or common daily life, often subject to the same sufferings and the same events as anybody else's, there is light and hope, because the Holy Spirit makes us aware of God our Father's care, full of love, for all of us, going beyond the limits of time and the present life.

We are disconcerted when Jesus tells us not to worry what happens to us, because God takes care of the birds and does not let them die of hunger, even though there are also disasters in birds' lives! But Jesus wants us to understand that God is paying attention to us; if he pays attention to the birds and the flowers of the field, he will pay all the more attention to us his children, human creatures. Of course this apparently does not change our lives, or the world. When we meet people suffering or who are rejected by society or physically handicapped, we understand the importance for them of discovering the joy of living, because beyond all their sufferings, there is something that has been given them for ever, life. Life which has been given to them by God, and can only have been given them for their own growth and satisfaction: every living being has this hope.

[3]Jn. 2:25
[4]Matt. 5:3–11

The most difficult and deep work that the Spirit can do in a heart is to give it the beginnings of happiness. When the Spirit gives the poor a glimpse of happiness, this is not of course to weaken their efforts to improve their position, or to set aside mankind's great struggle to transform the material and moral conditions of life, to share wealth out and abolish material poverty.

The beatitudes are in no way a discouragement to the efforts of love and justice. None of us would have the face to say that the poor are happy as they are. We are incapable of giving this happiness which only the Spirit can give, by making people aware that they are loved by God. Of course men can reveal God's love to one another, and some people's vocation is to show others how much God loves them. Some of Christ's more disconcerting statements can only be understood by the light of the Spirit. I do not feel capable of explaining the beatitudes to anyone. In many cases it is better to say nothing, because only the Holy Spirit can make them come alive in men's hearts.

The Word at work in us

The work of the Spirit—I was going to say the specific work of the Spirit sent by Jesus—is to make us discover God the Father through personal experience. The Spirit sent by Jesus glorified has a mission bound up with Christ's mission and following from it. Re-read John's gospel and if you have a concordance, take the trouble to look up all the passages in which Jesus speaks of the Spirit. This is very illuminating. Jesus is going to leave the world but he will send the Spirit. It is a bit like a 'change of government': Jesus was there but he will be so no longer. He was able to advise the apostles but he will no longer be able to do so in a human way, through words. They will no longer be able to ask him questions. They will not have the comfort of his physical human presence. But instead, something will happen in their hearts, something completely new: the reign of the Spirit sent by Jesus.[5]

Thus there is a profound unity between Jesus' mission and the Spirit's. Both are one and the same God. Paraclete and Word are one and the same God. If Jesus is one with his Father, he is also one with the Spirit. The Spirit's mission is a continuation of Christ's work whose aim was to reveal the Father. The Spirit brings to life God's word, personalizes it in each of us and makes it effective. The Word of God includes all the words spoken by God's messengers, all the teachings in human languages, and also all the events, all God's acts throughout history, which were done for our instruction. But above all, and definitively, it is the Person of Christ who is the Word itself made man.

God's Word has been given to us, not just to be understood, grasped by our minds and studied, but also to be lived by. It is light and life, it is a Word that should be active in us. Yesterday when I was reciting the Office, I found this passage from Deuteronomy: 'For this commandment which I command you this day is not too hard for you, neither is it far off. . . . But the word is very near you; it is in your mouth and in your heart, so that you can do it.'[6] Yes, God's Word transforms and gives us life but only if it is listened to, respected, assimilated and done. Otherwise it has no value. What would be the use of teaching the Word, what would be the use of teaching Scripture, what good would exegesis be, if their aim was not to receive into our hearts this Word which slowly transforms us because it is divine and because we do it? Did not Jesus tell the disciples this repeatedly? 'Do what I tell you. He who loves me is he who does my will.'[7] We must bring God's Word to life by doing it, otherwise it is a word which brings death to us: we have not accepted it as a word of God but as a powerless human word.

[5]Jn. 14
[6]Deut. 30:11–14
[7]Jn. 14:15 and 21

94

People nowadays think they have rediscovered the value of God's Word. But it would be a bit naïve to imagine that Christians waited for what is called the post-Vatican II era to live by the Gospel! From the beginning every single saint lived by it, this Word of the Gospel. However, in our time it has been rediscovered with new words because the need is felt for a certain renewal. But this has also happened throughout the ages.

Think simply of Brother Charles of Jesus: few saints paid so much attention to the Gospel, the Gospel received in an extreme simplicity of spirit and put into practice with great courage. The desire to make his life conform to the Gospel was the life force of all his prayers, all his meditations, whether they were written down or in silence in the presence of the Blessed Sacrament. He looked at Jesus and contemplated what he had said, what he had done and wondered how to imitate him. That was all but it was very demanding.

We sometimes find the Gospel too simple because we do not receive it as something to be lived. I sometimes feel disconcerted when some people try to deepen the Gospel by complicated, intellectual or over-scientific reflection. This does not take us very far because the intelligence we need for the Word of God in Scripture is the effort to discern God's intention in it. Yes, we must understand what God wants to tell us, what he said to us.

We must admit that in the past people went in for interpretations too far removed from the literal meaning, the true sense of Scripture, with symbolic and allegorical interpretations and what was called the 'spiritual sense'. In spite of this the Spirit made use of these interpretations even when they were deficient, because many Christians, even saints, drew spiritual nourishment from them. But our times are more realist, more objective and scientific and we should not regret it.

In fact it is a very good thing to make the effort to understand better the true meaning of what Jesus said, to grasp what he actually wanted to communicate to us. This search for the truth requires us to know about the environment Jesus lived and spoke in. Nevertheless, the object of our seeking should always be to discover Christ's intention, his thought which we must make our own in order to change our lives. Look at Francis of Assisi facing the Gospel: he took it literally, he lived it. The first attempts at theology were commentaries on Scripture, a commentary on the words of the Lord. Nowadays we are returning to this method because we feel the need for renewal and sound exegesis has made good progress. This is called biblical theology. It is a very good thing.

Yes, the Word of God is the manifestation of the Father. We should not be afraid because in Jesus Christ there is a *revelation*, that is to say that Jesus has removed a veil—the etymological sense of the word—and shown us inside the sanctuary of the Father's secret life. How? Simply by revealing himself, because he was the Son, he came from God and this secret life of God's was his own. We should not be afraid of the Word and the idea of 'revelation'. Nowadays we find a certain reticence in the use of this term which was used frequently in the past. Jesus himself used it: 'I thank thee, Father, Lord of heaven and earth, that thou hast hidden these things from the wise and understanding and revealed them to babes.'[8]

The Word of God in us is first of all light. How could we walk as God's children if he did not light our way? If God expects us to behave as his children, that is to say freely, if he expects us to love him, he must make us able to direct our own footsteps. The essential condition for freedom is the power of self-direction in the light of intelligence. Otherwise we are not free. We have to know ourselves well enough in order to decide how to act, we have to know ourselves well enough to be able to love. Without the light of truth this is not possible.

One of the most difficult tasks in the Church's mission today is to fulfil her claim truly to give us a knowledge of

[8]Matt. 11:25

God, knowledge of the mystery of Christ and his godhead. The Church also passes on to us all that the saints have perceived of this mystery throughout the centuries. All this knowledge about God is a treasure, a trust the Church must guard. How could a Christian get far on his journey without having a light in his heart, a light on God which is also a light on men, because the two are inseparable. The better I know Christ the more I discover and the better I respect the dignity of man. I do not believe that a light given us by the Holy Spirit to show us the Word of God can be authentic unless it also throws light on mankind. We must ask for this light of the Holy Spirit, seek it in prayer, and it will become knowledge, certainty of the truth and wisdom in us.

Of course I believe that we discover God through love, whenever we go to the limit of our power of loving. For light and love, light and strength are closely connected in the life of the Spirit, the life given to us by the Holy Spirit, because he is fire, he is light, he is love, he is truth, all indissolubly one because he is one God.

We could discuss endlessly how all this is possible. But first of all we must take account of one reality: there exists a human consciousness, a human intelligence, a human heart which have been initiated into the contemplation of the secret of God—the consciousness, heart and intelligence of Christ. Christ's incarnation was the unique and fundamental event which radically modified the relationship between God and man, the creator and the creature. From now on every human prayer is a sharing in this contemplation of the Father by Christ, because in him, in his heart, and only there, has this contemplation became communicable to other human beings. We cannot see God. No human creature has ever seen God, and that is why Christ's human sharing in the knowledge the Son has of the Father, is completely beyond us. But we know that Christ shared the secret by the very fact that he was God's eternal only Son and at the same time true Son of man. So there is a secret in Christ, a sort of obscure transfiguration of his

97

heart and mind. I am speaking of course of Christ during his life on earth, when he shared our earthly state. I do not mean Christ as he is now, living in the glory of the Father. Every christian prayer is thus a sharing, a communion, in Christ's prayer, not just the prayer by which he intercedes for us, but also the prayer with which he contemplates his Father. Here I am concerned chiefly with this contemplative prayer. So we must ask the question: in what way are we able to collaborate in this work which is pre-eminently the work of the Spirit in us?

There are successive layers in the spiritual life of every man and in the deeper ones the Spirit of God acts in a purer and freer way, because we cannot consciously reach them of our own accord. Prayer which has become contemplation comes from this depth. Prayer itself has several levels at which the action of the Spirit is also present but in a hidden and indiscernible way. Whereas when our prayer comes from a deeper level than our consciousness, the Holy Spirit sometimes reveals himself in the depths of the heart to which he communicates an unutterable knowledge and wisdom. Of course these contemplatives transmit a certain radiance, as in the case of Theresa of Avila or John of the Cross. If we pay close attention to these saints who experienced God in their hearts we will receive some light from them. But this radiance remains diffuse and mysterious. Whereas in other cases the Spirit does not mind dropping the sort of incognito in which he normally operates and leaves us with all our human responsibility to seek, make our own way, love.

The free gift of grace and the dry bread of contemplation

These are the laws of your life of prayer, worship of Christ's humanity and sharing in his prayer. You already know all this. Still when we are continually questioning our prayer, I sometimes wonder whether we have not forgotten these laws. For what is there so mysterious about our prayer? We sometimes tend to escape from the darkness of contemplation and seek a recipe or some magic solution to enable us to pray as we imagine we ought to pray. It is all much simpler: you have only to surrender to prayer. Do as Brother Charles did, take the Scriptures, listen to God, stay with him. What more can I tell you? Read the Gospel and you will see that Jesus repeatedly tells us to persevere, just persevere. This is the way of the Spirit but it is a hard way, precisely because it lies at the level where darkness and purification are more painful, or because we are tempted to give it all up since we can no longer feel our prayer which gives us the impression that we are not doing anything. But this is when the wholly gratuitous nature of contemplation becomes plain. You do nothing. It is very hard to accept because we would like to have some guarantee that we are praying, a guarantee that the Spirit is praying in us. We would like to be consoled by the Spirit. It is true that Jesus called him the Comforter, the Paraclete, but he does not comfort us in the way we expect. As St Paul said:[9] Children need soft sweet food, whereas the adult in the faith must eat the dry bread of pure and naked contemplation. Every way of prayer leads us at a certain point into the pathless desert and the dark night of faith. You can inquire of John of the Cross or Theresa of the Child Jesus on this subject. She is quite different from him and yet so similar. She expressed her experience of prayer in a different way which was closer to our own.

We must know that when we begin on the road of worship of God, the way of prayer, we must go to the very limits of ourselves. We cannot receive light from God without this light at the same time piercing us. We cannot know God without coming to see ourselves with new eyes. We are afraid of this self-discovery. There is no genuine prayer which is not also a deepening of love, which means a loss of self. So we instinctively draw back. A prayer which

[9] Heb. 5:12–14

remains on the level of a burst of enthusiasm or a new insight into the Gospel may satisfy us, because it is always a joy to see a new light. For when we walk in the darkness of love, love which Christ wants to be absolute and disinterested, it is much harder. I cannot tell you more and anyway it would be of no use to you. Do as Brother Charles of Jesus did: see how he prayed and do likewise. See how he persevered even though when he had reached a certain spiritual maturity he found himself in darkness and what he called total dryness of feeling.

Perhaps you are tempted to ask: 'But who will guarantee that all this is true?' I can prove nothing to you. However, I do not believe someone can reach this degree of darkness on the way of prayer—if this trial comes from the Lord—without receiving the strength and secret certainty which will prevent his giving up praying. We may have the impression that we are no longer praying, we may even be tempted to abandon everything, but deep down we know we are in God's hands. Jesus says that we cannot find our lives without losing ourselves. We must be prepared to lose ourselves, no longer to know where we are. We must accept this as a communion with the abandonment felt by Christ himself.

At the beginning of a life of prayer it is fairly normal to receive lights, consolations, joys, and we then have the tendency to think that everything is going well, we are making progress. We look through the writings of St John and St Theresa to see which 'castle of the soul' we have reached. We may not admit it because this would be lacking in humility. But we would like to be sure that we have been favoured with a true grace of prayer. The Lord will soon make all these feelings go away, because although this inner state is genuine, it commits us to go further along a harder way. We must go on, whatever happens, because it is during these moments of darkness that the Spirit of Jesus really reigns. Perhaps at this level of darkness the action of the Spirit is at its purest, because we are in a state in which we can do nothing without him. All this takes place beyond feelings, beyond words, beyond human explanations, beyond imagining: it is the work of the Spirit of God. But we are rarely tempted to glory in it because we feel so small, so weak and miserable. We feel we are no longer capable of anything and what is difficult to accept is that at this point in the road, we should leave everything to God.

Light of the Spirit and human wisdom

But there is also everyday life. At this level we must constantly take the initiative, there are always things to be done and decisions to be made. The initiatives of the Holy Spirit never free us from our ordinary human responsibility. The Spirit's initiatives accompany—I do not know how to put it—enliven and dynamize human action. The Spirit makes use of human needs, human talents and desires so that his constant action is somehow included in our freedom. That is why—I repeat—the divine action is usually indiscernible, except at certain moments when some inner compulsion or enlightenment has unforeseeably changed the direction of our lives. Perhaps you can remember the moment when an unexpected illumination marked the beginning of a conversion or a religious vocation. It does not matter that to onlookers this conversion or vocation may appear to be the result of a number of natural circumstances: a meeting, a disappointment, an intellectual journey, a trial endured.

This is also true of our growth in perfection, in putting the Gospel into practice. The Holy Spirit will not make up for our lack of generosity or indecision. Neither will his light dispense us from the necessary reflection to come to a better understanding of God's Word. We must try our hardest to understand it, study it, meditate on the Gospel, in order to discover as plainly as possible the objective meaning of Christ's words. This is also true of good works, even when we know we are doing them for God. Even when we are speaking of a charismatic action, like the founding of a religious order, the Spirit of God uses human means, human talents and character. Theresa of Avila who had many illuminations and signs from God or even appearances of the Lord telling her the foundations to be made in certain towns, never allowed herself to be guided by these divine inspirations alone. She waited till providential circumstances or decisions by authority showed her what she should do. She never abandoned common sense. This was wisdom!

Of course, different temperaments will see things in all kinds of different ways. Some people seem to want to wait for everything to come from God and when they run into a difficulty they say: 'The Lord will provide,' or 'God will sort it out,' or 'Pray and everything will be all right.' Sometimes they are annoying because what they say seems silly. We may wonder, 'If we believe in Providence, does that mean we should do nothing? Is it more perfect to say that God will provide?' No, we are never dispensed from making our own judgments, taking action, working. If we thought we were, this would be a false notion of the action of the Holy Spirit and God's universal Providence. Even when we think we have had an inspiration from God, we must not act against common sense, sound reason or obedience. But this does not mean that divine wisdom is not sometimes opposed—or rather transcendent—to the judgments of human wisdom. There are moments when the Holy Spirit urges us to leap in the dark. Some religious vocations and some enterprises may seem mad and unreasonable,[10] even though they were inspired by God. But this is another matter.

All that we have said about the action of the Spirit is equally applicable to the spiritual life of the Church and religious orders. It is quite easy for an historian to describe the history of a religious order without mentioning any intervention of the Holy Spirit. The birth of such an order

[10]I Cor. 4:10

102

met a need of the time; it was the result of a certain pattern of circumstances; it arose from the vision of its founder whose psychological motives the historian can investigate. It has even been possible to write a history of 'religous feeling', the Church's spirituality, the different movements in it and to discern their natural causes. And this all holds water!

The Holy Spirit does not come to upset the normal course of human life or the course of history. The Spirit walks with us, or rather, in our hearts. Later we will speak of the charismatic movements which seem to go against the course of history, even though it is possible to think they were caused by anger or bewilderment at a certain period.

To return to the saints, it is remarkable to see how God makes use of their temperaments, their talents, qualities and even their faults. You know the story of Charles de Foucauld. We could tell his story—and this has been done—ascribing his conversion and vocation to the historical circumstances in which he lived and his reactions to them. But for those who believe in his mission, it is obvious that he was impelled by the Holy Spirit who made use of all these circumstances and made his life a supernatural success. Can we imagine what would have happened if Brother Charles of Jesus had resisted the light? God alone knows what might have become of him. However, he would have still been the same man, influenced and formed by the same period, the same family background, the same temperament. He might even have engaged in the same activities, for his exploration of Morocco, which was a turning point in his life, was apparently undertaken for thoroughly unreligious motives.

Thus every man has different levels of life at which his freedom can operate. The higher we rise in the life of the Spirit the closer we come to the levels which are outside our control, where only the Spirit of Jesus can enlighten and transform us. That is why the knowledge of God takes us beyond ourselves. Our thirst to know God leads us to seek his face through contemplation which is the work of the Spirit alone. The same is true of charity because the light of faith and the power of love go together. The over-flowing charity of some saints is a manifest work of the Spirit which leads them to will and act beyond ordinary human power. In both of these, the understanding of the faith and the power of divine love in us, the Holy Spirit is ever active. For if God is love, there is no limit to loving, and there are times in our lives when we particularly need the power of his Spirit to be beyond ourselves. The same is true of hope when we are undergoing the sufferings of the cross. The beatitudes we have spoken of are dimensions of hope, hope which has repercussions in this world by giving us a happiness which the disciples of Jesus can enjoy here below. In fact hope which goes beyond the limits of human life is life's true meaning.

Jesus always kept his eyes fixed on the two stages of human life: earth and heaven. Sometimes he seems not to distinguish them. When Jesus refers to those who have left everything to follow him, Simon Peter protests: 'Lo, we have left everything and followed you. What then shall we have?'[11] Was Peter thinking about the restoration of the kingdom in Israel when he hoped to be repaid for his services by a position of power and dignity? Perhaps! For this question of Peter's reminds us of the request made to Jesus by the mother of the sons of Zebedee, which they had probably asked her to make for them: 'Command that these two sons of mine may sit, one at your right hand and one at your left, in your kingdom.'[12] Nothing could be clearer!

However, Jesus' answer to Simon Peter surprises us. He not only speaks of thrones on which they will sit to judge the twelve tribes of Israel, but says that they will receive far more than they have left and 'inherit eternal life'.[13] Jesus even says that they will receive 'a hundredfold now

[11]Matt. 19:27
[12]Matt. 20:21
[13]Matt. 19:29

in this time. . . .'[14] This is why the dimension of hope to which the Holy Spirit gives all his power and which, through his secret illumination, can even be a source of happiness in the midst of suffering, the darkness of the cross, is valid for this life too but would have no meaning if its fulfilment were not beyond, in the Kingdom of God to come. Likewise, the contemplation of God who is Truth would be meaningless if it were not fulfilled in the beatific vision. It is unthinkable that such contemplation of God's inner life begun here by the light of the Spirit could disappear. It is an already present reality of eternal life. Likewise it is obvious that the reflection of happiness that we can find in suffering is only meaningful with reference to a future fulfilment. Love goes on and will continue to go on because love, as St Paul says, remains itself.[15] That is why love is the greatest fulfilment of the divine life here below.

[14]Mk. 10:30
[15]'For now we see in a mirror dimly, but then face to face. Now I know in part; then I shall understand fully, even as I have been fully understood. So faith, hope and love abide, these three; but the greatest of these is love.' I Cor.13:12–13

VIII

The Spirit of Truth Which the World Cannot Receive

We have seen that the Spirit's task—if we may use such a word of the Spirit of God!—his mission, the work he must accomplish through human freedom, is the work of Christ himself. Jesus said to his apostles: 'I will send you the Spirit of truth.' So it is Jesus who sends the Spirit and tells us that he is truth.[1] When Pilate was interrogating him, Jesus told him that he had come into this world to bear witness to the truth, and the Holy Spirit bears witness to Jesus. 'He will bear witness to me.' It is the Spirit of Jesus who strengthens our faith and bears witness in our hearts that Jesus is the Son of God. This same Spirit bore witness in Simon Peter's heart when he confessed that Christ was God and that this was his true messianic mission. Furthermore, Jesus says the Spirit 'will glorify me'.[2]

We cannot read John chapters fourteen, fifteen and sixteen without being struck by the apostle's insistence on truth. The Spirit's mission is to guide people, to guide the disciples by enlightening them. When Jesus spoke thus to his apostles he was about to leave them, as they knew. Jesus told them: 'He will teach you all things, and bring to your remembrance all that I have said to you.'[3] This tells us that the action of the Spirit is a continuation of the

[1] Jn. 14:16–17 'But when the Counsellor comes, whom I shall send to you from the Father, he will bear witness to me.' Jn. 15:25
[2] Jn. 16:14
[3] Jn. 14:26

106

revelation in Christ of the Word as a divine Person made flesh. It is the same God who teaches, who reveals himself and acts in different ways, without contradiction. There is no contradiction possible in the development of the Kingdom from the seed planted by Jesus, because the Kingdom is also his.

This guidance by the Spirit is a new departure for humanity. He will remain with us forever. He is the Spirit of the one God, he is the Spirit who proceeds from the Father, as the Gospel tells us. He is also the Spirit of Jesus, in perfect unity with him, so that when Jesus says that the Spirit of Truth will remain with his disciples for ever, this is the same as saying: 'I am with you always, to the close of the age'[4] because Jesus remains with them by virtue of the reign of the Spirit.

Some of the things Jesus said may surprise us, as for example: 'The Spirit will teach you all things.' What does he mean by 'all things'? But these words remind us of another saying of Jesus: 'Without me you can do nothing.' Both these statements sound absolute. We must be aware that this 'totality' that the Spirit teaches us means the whole of the revelation made by Christ. It means 'all the things' that Jesus wants to tell us from and about his Father, 'all the things' concerning wisdom which derive from this contemplation of the truth, wisdom which will be like a projection of this truth into our humble human daily lives. And it is in this sphere of divine truth that we can do nothing without Christ. Without him we cannot know the Father; without Christ we cannot go beyond a certain limit in our conception of human life. Without Christ there is a mystery about human beings which we cannot wholly grasp. Without him we cannot enter God's secrets. And without Christ could we have the faith and hope to live as children of God in this world? In the same passage of the Gospel where Jesus says without him we can do nothing,

[4]Matt. 28:20

107

he tells us the parable of the vine whose branches we are.[5] He is the vine, his disciples are the branches which must be joined to him or they will die; if they are cut off from the trunk they can no longer be his disciples.

When Jesus tells us that the eternal life he came to bring us is fed by the bread of life, which he is himself, he is also telling us about the close communion between our beings, flesh and spirit and his own. Of course this is difficult to understand or even admit. He said 'I am the Truth'; he said 'I am the Life'. This does not mean our biological life, our natural animal life, but the life of the Spirit. If we want to understand Jesus' message and the reign of the Spirit, we must have an idea of human nature which gives an important place to the spirit. Otherwise we cannot understand the realities Jesus is talking about.

In our deepest selves there is something that awaits the glory of God. It is only in this depth of human nature that Jesus can sow his Word, it is here his transfigured humanity, body and blood, given for us, can reach us and the Word of God can feed us.[6]

Two irreconcilable views?

We asked whether faith in Christ involved a reaching up of man towards God, in worship and self-abasement at God's greatness, or whether faith was a proclamation of human dignity. Current theological research tends to stress the latter, the dignity of man and his earthly destiny. This is true. But we should not set the one against the other, because man without Christ is nothing; without Christ, whatever our view of man and his history, death will have the last word and generations of human beings will be finally conquered by it. Thus it is true to say that without Christ we are nothing compared to what we are with him;

[5]Jn. 15:1–6
[6]Jn. 6:34–65

108

with him we are everything because he has eternal life and he has conquered death. He who has the Father has everything. It is difficult to explain in a rational way why we should be united to Jesus like the branches to the vine, because we are talking about sharing the life of the glorified Christ. So what is this life? Not just animal life, but the life of mind and spirit? Life is knowing, life is loving, life is action, life is fertility. All this is true of Christ but not in the sphere of visible things available to our senses.

We must say a word about the Church, because the Church is also like a vine whose branches we are. We cannot remain united to Christ without remaining united with the Church. Neither can we reduce this bond between the vine and its branches to a visible relationship with a structured hierarchical Church. The Church also possesses a mystery of life which is beyond definition. It is always Christ's.

Now we understand why the Spirit cannot be in the world. When Jesus spoke of this Spirit of truth, he said that the world was incapable of receiving him because it did not see him or know him.[7] He is a Spirit of life, a Spirit of love, a Spirit of freedom and we can only know him if we let ourselves be guided by him. Jesus says the world cannot see him because what is needed here is inner vision, a contemplative certainty. Obviously such a vision of the Spirit can only exist in the heart of man, not in the world. 'You know him, for he dwells with you, and will be in you.'[8] 'You know him because you have received the Word into your hearts and you are my disciples . . . that where I am you may be also.'[9] 'He who has ears to hear, let him hear,' Jesus would add, as he so often did.[10]

[7]Jn. 14:17
[8]Jn. 14:17
[9]Jn. 14:3
[10]Matt. 11:5;13:9 and 43; Mk. 4:9,23; 7:16; Lk. 8:8; 14:35

Two inseparable views

We could sum up the reign of the Spirit, who is also the Spirit of Jesus, by saying that he has come to enlighten, complete, deepen and adapt to each individual human life, personalize, if we may so put it, the revelation made to us in Jesus Christ which we have accepted into our hearts by faith. He has come to enable us to live our lives as Jesus wants us to live them. For Jesus has his own idea about man and his relationships in society. He has his own view about how human beings should live. He tells us about it in his teachings and constantly repeats: 'If you love me, do as I tell you. Live as I have said.' Hence the extreme importance of Scripture, the Word of the Lord. Without it the light of the Spirit would find no way into our minds.

In order to teach us the Spirit needs Jesus' words which sustain his light, he needs Jesus' words and ideas and silently brings them to life in his own way. The Spirit does not work like a human being. Jesus spoke to us, Jesus communicated a wisdom to us, the knowledge he had of his Father. He communicated it to us by the way of knowledge and love which a human heart can use and understand. But the Spirit acts differently, the Spirit needs the material of the life, acts and teachings of Christ. Jesus said many things to his apostles, although they could not understand them all. Jesus said some things so deep that people will never cease to inquire into them and find in them a living force, a clarity of truth which is ever new and inexhaustible.

Jesus' words are simple but they are truth and life. Whether we want to understand the truth of them or experience the love in them in our own lives, we need the Spirit. This is where the Spirit acts, gives us light on the revelation made to us by Jesus.

That is why when I spoke to you about prayer and worship, I reminded you that Brother Charles, like all contemplatives, always took as his starting point the life and words of the Lord in the Gospel. There is no better way for us to advance in the light of the Spirit sent by the Father than to try and feel in our lives the power of Jesus' words. Thus there is an indissoluble link between the revelation in Jesus Christ and the reign of the Spirit. These two realities are so inseparable that the one is incomprehensible without the other. It is a mistake to speak constantly about the work of the Spirit without reference to Christ. What would the reign of the Spirit be without him? It could not be a new revelation as if we could do without Christ, his Gospel and the manifestation of the Father in Jesus. The Spirit can say nothing of himself. He can only act through the words, actions and manifestations of God in Jesus. Nothing can happen between God and us except through the glorified humanity of the Son of man.

How to receive the Spirit

I would like to say something else. In Jesus' words there is an assurance of truth that we cannot forget; it stands out but cannot be proved. It is the foundation of our faith. Jesus is true, Jesus is Truth. The word truth has meaning for men in any language even when philosophies discuss endlessly the notion of Truth. We may be sceptical, especially about realities we can neither see nor prove, we may be eclectic and say that after all there is not only one truth, but a multitude of half-truths or provisional truths. Pilate's words are sceptical and bored: 'What is Truth?' in answer to Jesus' saying: 'For this I was born and for this I have come into the world, to bear witness to the Truth.'[11] Jesus is about to die for it. Pilate evades the issue and refuses to continue the conversation.

I am afraid that many people who are drawn to Christ by their need for truth are incapable of receiving Christ's truth in its simplicity. However, we must accept it totally. He said he was the Son of God. What he said is true. He

[11]Jn. 18:37

111

himself is absolutely true, as true as my own life, as true as the material universe. Christ is true. He speaks the truth, he does not speak in symbols or half-truths. He spoke the truth and this truth is the foundation of our faith. What other foundation could there be? Among the prayers recommended for the faithful in certain missals there was an act of faith which said we believe in God because he 'can neither be mistaken nor deceive us.'

Of course it is possible to sow doubt about the truth of Christ and his godhead. Human sciences can always shake realities like these. Our faith goes back to the apostles' faith. We believe that their faith was true because it was faith in someone they had seen, heard and loved. Who could contradict them by saying Jesus was untrue? It was because they believed that Jesus was true that they confessed with all their heart: 'To whom shall we go . . . you are the Holy One of God.'[12] The truth of the faith is sure, for the faith is true. It is not just a vague feeling. God cannot deceive us. God does not play games with us. Christ does not play games with us. What he said is serious and important because it is the truth, totally true. He died as a testimony to his Truth.

So when we are asked, as we frequently are nowadays: 'Who is Jesus Christ?' we too must answer truly, in full awareness of Christ's truth. I showed you how the way to faith for the people who had come to Christ, the Jews and especially the apostles, was a difficult one. Jesus was very reticent about himself so that the crowds would not treat him like the earthly Messiah they expected. But he was not as reticent when he stood before his judge, because he was about to die and the fulfilment of his mission was imminent. Then he said: 'Yes, I am the Son of God, I am the Messiah and you will see him return in glory and you will be with him.' In this his last hour there was no more mystery in Jesus' words but a clear statement.

Likewise when people ask us about Jesus Christ, they

[12]Jn. 6:68

112

are seeking something and perhaps they are not ready to let the Word of God and the light of Truth into their hearts and minds. But as for us, we must confess Jesus Christ and say that for us he is God, he is God's only Son, manifested in truth and in the glory of his resurrection. The Spirit Jesus sent is in us, for he cannot act and enlighten unless he finds a heart and mind ready to receive him.

We should not imagine that the Spirit sent by Jesus can work outside a human heart. Where else could he act? He is not the Destiny of History. No, the Spirit Jesus spoke of is clearly a Spirit who acts in our hearts. 'He is in you,'[13] Jesus said to his disciples. That is why the world cannot receive him, for the conditions for receiving him are only satisfied by Christ's disciples.

In order to receive the Spirit we must give him freedom of action. This needs true humility and welcoming faith. It needs a thirst for truth, all truth, and readiness to receive it whatever it may be or whatever the consequences. Pride of mind is one of the chief obstacles to the reign of the Spirit. We also need freedom of will, because the Spirit does not give us an abstract theoretical knowledge but the knowledge of God which cannot operate without love. If we are not capable of accepting the demands of love as God reveals them to us, neither are we capable of accepting the light of the Spirit. A light which did not involve the transformation of our lives would not be a lasting light. That is why we are all more or less closed against the action of the Spirit. No one is perfectly open to the Holy Spirit. We must realize that the fundamental requirement in our approach to Christ and in the disciples' lives is readiness to fulfil the conditions necessary to receiving the Spirit. 'You know him,' said Jesus.[14] Yes, the disciples knew him because all that Jesus had done and said enabled them to know him. But do we know him? We know him to the extent that we know Jesus, and we know Jesus to the

[13]Jn. 14:17
[14]Ibid

113

extent that we know his Spirit. That is why this divine knowledge is a gift, like a leap into a closed circle which has no rational door. This requires from us an attitude of confident surrender to our God.

A right notion of history

I return to the question of the Spirit's presence in the world. How can the Spirit be in the world? What is this 'world' that Jesus speaks of? It is difficult to define: it is something made by man. The world is what makes mankind be as it is, and at the same time mankind is a slave to the world. The world is an attitude, the interdependence of people, it is imposed on individuals, it is a collective way of thinking and acting, often evil. The world is a reality produced by people living collectively. It is a reality in which evil too often appears. In the world there is a reign of evil, a reign of error, a reign of sin, as there is also a reign of justice and a tension to struggle free from evil. In the world evil in some sense escapes individual responsibility. In a true sense it reigns. When you read John's gospel you find that when Jesus speaks of the Spirit of truth he is contrasting it with the spirit of lying, the spirit of error. It is difficult to speak of this without being accused of 'manicheism', that is to say believing in a struggle in mankind between the power of Truth and the power of Error with a capital E, between good and evil, between something or someone Christ calls 'the Prince of this world' and the Spirit of God. Although our formulations may be clumsy, we are speaking of a mysterious reality.

This is how Jesus sees human life. The Spirit of truth whom Jesus promises and gives, is a Spirit that the world cannot receive. The world cannot receive the Spirit because this Spirit of truth and love can only be received by a heart and mind and not by a collectivity. There is not one single action of the Spirit sent by Jesus that takes place outside human hearts.

How is this possible? How is it that this reign of the Spirit does not also concern the world? We ask this when we see people living together, organizing, struggling, thinking, making plans, rebelling, making war, seeking, if necessary by violence, to make certain ideologies prevail, at the cost of continual upheavals or even bloody revolutions, and all because they want to live in peace, to live a more just or comfortable human life on earth. Everyone has his own plan for the new society, plans in which one fails to see where the Spirit could intervene, except in every human mind and heart.

Nevertheless, God has a plan for the whole of history. When I spoke of Providence which governs the world, I said that this word is not often used now. The idea is no longer familiar even to Christians. There are all sorts of reasons for this. We are living at a time when people have become aware that certain words are outworn. They are replaced by new words which will doubtless wear out even faster. But we must go beyond words and know what is being talked about. The idea of Providence implied a certain view of God's intervention even in the private life of every man in a universe whose happenings are ordered by the divine mind and will. Hence man's feeling of dependence on God's plan; of being in God's hands. This notion is unacceptable to modern man who is more aware of his own responsibility. He feels he depends only on himself and the future of mankind will be what he makes it. This notion is just as true as the former one, even though they are usually seen as contradictory. But now we tend to speak rather of the unfolding of God's plan than of a paternalist Providence. The need is felt to discover this plan inscribed in the laws of evolution. Man has become aware of the dynamism of his history, of the continual change which he calls progress. He is more interested in what his future and the future of society will be.

We are convinced that God has a plan for the world and mankind. But how can we discover it? Christians themselves want to know this plan in order to serve it and work with it in so far as they are called to do so. Yes, God has a plan which includes all things, the final destiny of mankind, all history. But no one can discover this plan by looking at the course of history or the unforeseeable acts of freedom done by men who also make history. It is futile and impossible to think that we could discover God's plans at this level! We know nothing about the end of history except what Jesus allowed us to glimpse to give us a foundation for our hope. He spoke about eternal life and resurrection, but he did not speak about the historical forms of mankind's destiny, or even how it will end, because when Jesus speaks about eternal life and resurrection this is beyond the history of the world.

However, if God has a plan for our history, we know that this plan can only be loving and just. Of this we are certain and is not that enough to guide our taking part in evolution and the progress of mankind? Let us be content with what we are sure of. It is enough to make a disciple of Christ who knows he is God's son and every human being's brother, feel obliged to work constantly to improve the human condition, and bring about a society which is better suited to the dignity of people who are God's children and one another's brothers and sisters.

This society must thus be a fraternal society, a society of communion. Christians can be sure of their commitment to this. But we also know that in spite of people's efforts, no definite political plan will ever fulfil the ideal in a stable and final way. None of these plans can ever be regarded as an absolute, even if they are made in the name of the Gospel. We will always have to work to bring about more brotherhood, peace and justice. There is no end to it. In the light of a sound interpretation of the Gospel, every Christian must play his part. It is only too probable that mankind is going to run into increasing difficulties in the future.

Realities which 'profit nothing'

The action of the Spirit of God, even if it affects political works and plans, is upon the heart of man to free him for love. This is where the Spirit acts. Nowadays collectivity tends to dominate societies more and more and to threaten individual freedom and autonomy. This creates obstacles to people's growth in the Spirit of freedom and truth.

In this light it is common to hear certain forms of religious life being accused of uselessness to society. All christian believers are also accused that their faith is useless. For what use is a contemplative life to the task of creating a new society? To this question I reply: 'You speak of society. But what exactly do you mean by this word "society"? An economic structure, a certain ideology or political system? Or the community of people living together? And if we are speaking of people, should not the first question be: "What do they need? What do they want?" However you organize society politically and economically, one day people will ask themselves the meaning of life. I do not mention the meaning of death, because death is a reality we do not talk about much nowadays.'

Human beings have a deep need for realities which 'profit nothing', except to give them inner peace and true happiness, such as pure love does. This is a bit like the arts, music in particular. What use is it? In what way does a violinist contribute to the creation of society? In no way, unless we reduce this music, as some do, to nothing but the expression of an ideology! I have taken music as an example because it is the purest art form, which expresses the unutterable. It is also the most universal because it brings people into communion beyond their language differences.

The religious life, the spiritual life, prayer and contemplation are not in fact directly useful to any political project, but we need them as much as we need bread. The world pretends it can do without religion, but it remains a light which must not be put under a bushel.

117